MW00616458

'Your company's speed of learning is what sets you apart from the competition. It is your moat and this book is how you create it.'
Lauren Cunningham, Learning and Development Manager, Bumble

'This book is exactly what L&D professionals need right now. It has broken the mould of "how to" learning books with Nelson Sivalingam applying a unique lens of entrepreneurship and startup strategies. A must have for any "learningpreneur" or intrapreneur. This is a seminal book of our times.'
Rustica Lamb, CEO and Founder, Bloom Learning Technologies

'This book captures sustainable shifts to a more appropriate, effective L&D function, better suited to the businesses of today and the future. I was particularly impressed with Nelson Sivalingam for grabbing the lessons learned and best bits from the disciplines of marketing, digital agencies and startups to bring their speed into the L&D sphere. Taking L&Ders beyond the buzzwords, he really understands agile, lean and design thinking in a way many L&Ders feel overwhelmed by. With practical suggestions, a myriad of story examples, support to build a new learning ecosystem and more, this book really is a must-read for modern L&Ders in business.'
Michelle Parry-Slater, Learning and Development Director, Kairos Modern Learning

Learning at Speed

*How to upskill and reskill your workforce
at pace to drive business performance*

Nelson Sivalingam

KoganPage

Publisher's note

Every possible effort has been made to ensure that the information contained in this book is accurate at the time of going to press, and the publishers and author cannot accept responsibility for any errors or omissions, however caused. No responsibility for loss or damage occasioned to any person acting, or refraining from action, as a result of the material in this publication can be accepted by the editor, the publisher or the author.

First published in Great Britain and the United States in 2022 by Kogan Page Limited

Apart from any fair dealing for the purposes of research or private study, or criticism or review, as permitted under the Copyright, Designs and Patents Act 1988, this publication may only be reproduced, stored or transmitted, in any form or by any means, with the prior permission in writing of the publishers, or in the case of reprographic reproduction in accordance with the terms and licences issued by the CLA. Enquiries concerning reproduction outside these terms should be sent to the publishers at the undermentioned addresses:

2nd Floor, 45 Gee Street
London
EC1V 3RS
United Kingdom
www.koganpage.com

8 W 38th Street, Suite 902
New York, NY 10018
USA

4737/23 Ansari Road
Daryaganj
New Delhi 110002
India

Kogan Page books are printed on paper from sustainable forests.

© Nelson Sivalingam, 2022

The right of Nelson Sivalingam to be identified as the author of this work has been asserted by him in accordance with the Copyright, Designs and Patents Act 1988.

ISBNs

Hardback   978 1 3986 0312 7
Paperback   978 1 3986 0310 3
Ebook   978 1 3986 0311 0

British Library Cataloguing-in-Publication Data
A CIP record for this book is available from the British Library.

Library of Congress Cataloging-in-Publication Data
Names: Sivalingam, Nelson, author.
Title: Learning at speed: how to upskill and reskill your workforce at
   pace to drive business performance / Nelson Sivalingam.
Description: London; New York, NY: Kogan Page, 2022. | Includes
   bibliographical references and index.
Identifiers: LCCN 2022009076 (print) | LCCN 2022009077 (ebook) | ISBN
   9781398603103 (paperback) | ISBN 9781398603127 (hardback) | ISBN
   9781398603110 (ebook)
Subjects: LCSH: Organizational learning. | Employees–Training of.
Classification: LCC HD58.82 .S588 2022 (print) | LCC HD58.82 (ebook) |
   DDC 658.3/124–dc23/eng/20220303
LC record available at https://lccn.loc.gov/2022009076
LC ebook record available at https://lccn.loc.gov/2022009077

Typeset by Integra Software Services, Pondicherry
Print production managed by Jellyfish
Printed and bound by CPI Group (UK) Ltd, Croydon, CR0 4YY

To Amma, Appa and Iram
for the life, love and lessons.

CONTENTS

Acknowledgements xi
About the author xiii

Introduction: Fastest learner wins 1

PART ONE
On your mark

01 **Where L&D is going wrong and how Lean can fix it** 11
Why L&D is like a failing startup 12
The three types of learning culture 14
What is Lean Learning and why does it matter? 16
What next? 18
References 18

02 **How to think Lean Learning before you do it** 21
The Lean Learning mindset 22
What next? 37
References 37

PART TWO
Get set

03 **Find the right business problem to solve** 41
Are you solving the right problem? 42
What are jobs to be done? 43
The customer discovery process 46
Get out of the building (or away from your desk) 52
What next? 55
References 56

04 Create an L&D strategy with the Learning Canvas 57

What if Elon Musk was an L&D professional? 58
How to create your Learning Canvas 61
What next? 71
References 73

05 Build a dynamic learning ecosystem 75

From static library to dynamic ecosystem 76
Open learning resources 77
Collaborative learning and knowledge sharing 78
Job aids and performance support 81
Coaching and mentoring 83
Online courses 86
Radically flipped classrooms 87
What next? 88
References 89

06 Personalize learning at scale 91

Organization-driven 'push' learning 92
Employee-driven 'pull' learning 94
Push or pull? That is not the question 97
What next? 98
References 99

07 Shape performance in the moments that matter 101

What is a moment that matters? 102
The types of moments that matter 103
Six influencers of moments that matters 103
What next? 110
References 110

08 Measure the proof of impact 111

Proof of knowledge 112
Proof of skill 113
Proof of performance 115

What next? 119
References 120

PART THREE
Go

09 Start testing with your Minimum Valuable Learning 123

What is (and isn't) a Minimum Valuable Learning 124
The benefits of starting with an MVL 125
The pitfalls to avoid when building an MVL 127
How to design an MVL that hits the bullseye 128
What next? 135
References 136

10 Achieve Learning-Challenge Fit or iterate trying 137

What is Learning-Challenge Fit? 138
How to achieve Learning-Challenge Fit 139
The Learning Flywheel 140
How to turn the flywheel faster 145
What next? 153
References 153

11 Deliver continuous learning with sprints 155

The Lean Learning sprint and what it's good for 156
Assemble the right team for the sprint 158
How to run a Lean Learning sprint 160
What next? 173
References 173

12 Scale your learning impact with marketing 175

How the L&D marketing funnel works 176
Building a learning brand 179
Putting social media to work 186
Influencer marketing 189
Search engine optimization (SEO) 192

Product positioning 195
Calls to action (CTAs) 197
Nudge marketing 198
What next? 202
References 202

Conclusion: Always winning 205

Index 211

ACKNOWLEDGEMENTS

Words don't seem enough to thank Iram Zahid, my best friend, high school sweetheart, and wife (by the time this book comes out). The other half to my everything. There is a lifetime of reasons for why I need to thank her, but this thank you is for putting up with me. While I shirked on my chores, missed date nights and spent almost every waking hour running the business and getting this book done, Iram made sure our lives continued to move forward. You have this book because of her.

Thank you to Appa and Amma – my parents. I thank them for the risks they took that gave me opportunities they never had and for giving me the safe space to take my own risks. I'm eternally grateful for their unwavering belief in everything I choose to do. My love for books and writing comes from growing up watching Appa lose himself in books and writing until the early hours, even when he had work the next day. Now he can read a book his son wrote.

This book is a product of my experiences building businesses for more than a decade, and I couldn't have done that without my brother and co-founder, Kuvera Sivalingam. The ups are better, and the downs are tolerable because I have him by my side. I thank him for making this journey what it is. With my lifestyle, I would have been a lot unhealthier today if it weren't for my younger brother and personal trainer, Antony Sivalingam. I owe him for my six-pack!

They say friends are the family you choose. I don't know who said that, but it's true for me. My life would be a lot duller, and I would be a far less rounded person without them. Thank you to the 'primaries': Kartik Bharadia, Jaina Bharadia, Suneet Chavda, Meena Gorecha, Qasim Bharmal, Jumana Bharmal, Milan Nanalal, Bhavini Patel; and the 'little primaries': Adam, Aarya and Sarrah. I thank them for always being there to celebrate my wins as their own. Thank you to my dear friends: Samiya Sayed for being my cheerleader from school and Jayshree Viswanathan for being my first reader.

Thank you to my co-founder and friend Ashish Kumar. I'm incredibly grateful he decided to go on this wild startup journey with me. Thank you to Jon Magnus, Lulu Dermeche, Hardik Jain, Chirag Paryani and Aaron-Spencer Charles for believing in HowNow when we were just getting started. Thank you to Amar Prasher for helping us get the first version of our product built.

Thank you to my amazing team at HowNow for making the company the success it is today and the adventure so much more fun. My gratitude to our customers for believing in HowNow and giving me the opportunity to learn from them. Thank you to our early investors, James Raj, Josephine Raj, Mark Pearson, Michael Whitfield and Chris Bruce, for their leap of faith.

Thank you to my editor Anne-Marie Heeney for being patient and supportive, and the Kogan Page publishing team for all the help along the way. Thank you to Sid Ahmed for spending hours on cover ideas.

Thank you to the frontline workers who kept the world going while I could sit in the comfort of my home to write: the baristas who made my much-needed coffees, the delivery drivers who kept me fed and the volunteers who got me and my family vaccinated.

Thank you to my beautiful little Eva for the face licks, sofa cuddles and for giving me a reason to get out of the house.

Last but far from least, **thank you** for reading this book.

ABOUT THE AUTHOR

Nelson Sivalingam is a serial entrepreneur, filmmaker, podcast host and future of work innovator. He is currently the CEO and Co-Founder at HowNow, one of the fastest-growing learning technology companies, with customers including tech unicorns GymShark and Checkout.com and global enterprises such as Telenor, Sanofi and Investec to name a few. As mentioned by Forbes and TechCrunch, HowNow is one of the edtech companies to watch out for.

Nelson is a regular speaker at events such as Learning Technologies, HRD Summit, AI Talks, Google Campus and London Tech Week, and in many of these cases it has been about the methodologies discussed in *Learning at Speed*. He is an ambassador and mentor for Startup Britain and a Guest Lecturer on Entrepreneurship.

Nelson has been recognized by Virgin Media Business as one of the top 30 young innovative founders in the country as well as one of the top Asian Stars in Tech by KPMG. He is a thought leader on Startups, Technology and Workplace Learning, contributing to publications such as the *Guardian*, the *Telegraph*, Startups.co.uk and *People Management*, and he was recently featured in Bloomberg's documentary on the Entrepreneurial Mindset.

Introduction: Fastest learner wins

The only way to win is to learn faster than anyone else.
ERIC RIES, AUTHOR OF *THE LEAN STARTUP*

In 2020, the 118-year-old Arcadia Group collapsed into administration. Faced with competition from newer names with slicker digital operations, the fashion retailer struggled to keep up. And then Covid-19 happened. If you haven't heard by now, it was 'unprecedented'. So much so, it was unprecedented how many times the word 'unprecedented' was used. With the global pandemic, Arcadia's cracks became chasms, putting the final nail in the coffin of the retail giant.

However, in the same year, the online fashion retailer ASOS turned 20 years old, quadrupled profits, added 3 million customers and bought Topshop and Miss Selfridge brands from Sir Philip Green's fallen fashion empire (Sweney and Butler, 2021). We're living in an era of exponential change, where new winners and losers are being made at remarkable speed. The accelerating pace of change creates uncertainties and opportunities. The fastest learners can seize the opportunities and win. Others who can't learn fast enough struggle to keep up, compete and eventually lose. *Learning at Speed* is your playbook for becoming the fastest learner.

Speed of learning is your moat

Amid the disruption of the Covid-19 pandemic, the fastest learners loomed larger than ever: developing vaccines at record speed, providing technology for remote schooling and working, and keeping millions of people fed, clothed, entertained, and in touch. But the world was changing fast even before the pandemic. Earlier it took a company in the Fortune 500, on average, 20 years to reach a billion-dollar valuation. Today it takes less than five. Whilst companies on the S&P 500 stock market index once lasted 65 years, today, they last an average of 15 (Viguerie et al, 2021). It took Microsoft 44 years to get to a trillion-dollar market cap. It took Bitcoin only 12.

The rate of change has destroyed all the traditional moats an organization once considered essential. It is no longer enough to have the highest-quality product, the cheapest price or the best people. Neither is it enough to 'just' learn. If you're not learning, you're not even in the race. But to win, organizations and individuals must learn to *learn at speed*. They must build the capability to rapidly unlearn old ways and learn new ones based on the ever-changing environment.

The World Economic Forum projects that by 2022 at least 54 per cent of all employees will need reskilling and upskilling to respond to changing work requirements (Brende, 2019). The window of opportunity to reskill and upskill is rapidly getting shorter, with 50 per cent of workers remaining in their roles requiring reskilling, given that 40 per cent of their core skills will change in the next five years.

Speed of learning is your organization's competitive advantage. The faster your workforce can learn and apply what they learn, the more likely your company will win. But how do you identify the skills they need to learn? How do you help your people learn those skills? How do you make sure those skills help improve business performance? And how do you keep doing all of that over and over again – fast enough to be the disruptor rather than the disrupted? These are just a few of the questions this book will answer.

Learning to learn fast from startups

Why startups? Because startups and the entrepreneurs who run them are agile, problem-solving machines that fail fast, learn fast – and put limited resources to drive maximum impact, fast. Startups are intentionally designed to grow quickly amidst uncertainty. What's the right product for the market? What's the right path to customers? What if Google builds a competitor? With so many questions to figure out the answers to and a dwindling runway of cash, startups have to learn fast, not just to survive but to thrive in a competitive market against all odds.

History shows that crises are startup incubators. Some of today's most prominent companies were launched during and shortly after the 2008 economic crisis, including Venmo, Uber, Credit Karma, Slack, WhatsApp and Groupon. Despite economic uncertainty and a volatile market, the Covid-19 pandemic has also led to a surge in startups. More businesses are being launched than at any time in the past decade, and existing startups are showing a rapid acceleration.

Market opportunities have opened up for businesses of all sizes to meet the new demand. However, the fast-paced, agile, learn/pivot ethos of many early-stage companies has meant they have been able to move faster to make the most of the opportunity. For example, beverage brand BrewDog started making hand sanitizers, restaurant-booking platform Resy embraced takeouts and deliveries, and fitness class subscription ClassPass revived and ramped up their live online classes.

The most successful startups are often the fastest learners and disrupt entire industries – and win. Suppose we assume the rate of change will not slow down. To win in ever-changing and even turbulent times, organizations must focus on building a more agile workforce, be open to experimentation, and be capable of learning from mistakes fast. These are all hallmarks of successful startups, and that's not by accident. The startup community has developed methodologies to learn at speed and win by design, which is at the heart of this book.

Why this book?

Before founding HowNow, one of the fastest-growing learning technology companies globally, I had never worked in Learning and Development. My only experience of L&D was feeling like a victim of awful training in my short corporate career. After which, I spent a decade building businesses: four to be precise. Failed one, sold one, pivoted one and now globally scaling one. From video advertising to film production to hospitality, I had developed a habit of building disruptive businesses in spaces I previously knew nothing about.

The experience taught me to look out for similarities between seemingly different domains. So when we first started implementing HowNow at some of the biggest companies in the world, I realized that many of the reasons that L&D was failing were similar to why startups fail. Building products no one wants, making big bets based on loaded assumptions rather than iteratively testing, and wasting resources on things that didn't solve the customer's problem.

We didn't want just to sell organizations a learning platform. We wanted to support them in building an impactful learning culture. So I adapted the greatest hits of Lean Startup, Agile Engineering and Customer Development to help L&D overcome their challenges. The response was brilliant. Many L&D leaders knew the buzzwords – agile, lean, design thinking – but they struggled to implement these philosophies, so they just reverted to how they'd always done things.

My adaptation of practical frameworks used by startups to build successful products whilst minimizing waste helped L&D put theory into practice. In true startup fashion, the methodologies in this book have been iterated and refined with every implementation. Along the way, I called this approach to deliver better learning aligned to business goals faster, *Lean Learning*. This book is a step-by-step guide for implementing Lean Learning in your organization. If something didn't work, it's not in this book – the result: a playbook that works.

Who is this book for?

Learning at Speed is for L&D professionals and every variation of that role: people development, talent development, performance consultants. The semantics of the job title don't matter as long as the WHY and HOW are the same. If you believe L&D should have a seat at the executive table and should play a role in shaping business performance through their work, then this book is for you.

This book is also for people managers, because building a fast-learning organization is not one department's job. It's every manager's job. In his influential book *High Output Management*, the former Intel CEO Andy Grove argues that maximizing output is achieved by focusing on tasks with high leverage: an activity that generates a high output level (Grove, 1995). Enabling your team to learn at speed is the highest-leverage activity a manager can do to increase the team's output, because learning applied is profit.

How this book is organized

In Part One of the book, we'll look at where L&D is going wrong and how Lean Learning can fix it. You'll discover the mindset shifts required to put Lean Learning into practice in your organization.

In Part Two, we'll look at how you can identify, understand and define the right business challenges to solve. You'll learn how to use the Learning Canvas to create your learning strategy collaboratively and quickly. Next, we'll cover how you can turn your strategy into tangible learning experiences, from how to build a dynamic learning ecosystem and personalize learning at scale, to delivering learning in the moments that shape performance and embedding measurement into your learning experiences to generate proof of impact.

In Part Three, you'll learn how to systematically start testing your strategy with Minimum Valuable Learning and iterate until you achieve Learning-Challenge Fit, all while maximizing impact and minimizing waste along the way. Discover how you can bring the entire process into a short Lean Learning sprint. Then, once you've got a learning strategy that solves the business challenge, learn how to use marketing to scale your impact.

Now is the time

If you're thinking, 'Can't we just shorten the courses we make so people can learn *faster?*', I'm afraid that won't cut it. When change is exponential, incremental improvements in a linear fashion aren't enough to keep up, let alone get ahead. Standing still or moving slowly is going backwards. The new world of work requires a whole new approach. Learning at speed is the future of work.

'But I'm not sure if my company is ready for this.' This is the most common concern I hear when I speak to L&D professionals. Ironically, that's a learning problem. My response back is, if not now, then when? We tend to underestimate exponential change. Psychologists call it 'exponential growth bias' (ETH Zurich, 2020). A spate of studies have shown that people susceptible to the exponential growth bias underestimate Covid-19 spread and are likely to perceive measures such as mask wearing, social distancing, or working from home as exaggerated.

Similar studies show that this phenomenon extends to many people underestimating the compound growth of savings, pension schemes and loans. When organizations underestimate the rate of change, they risk irreversible damage. The longer organizations take to build their capacity to learn at speed, the higher the risk of falling so far behind that it's too difficult to make up for lost ground.

Change is inevitable but learning at speed is intentional. This book is only a part of the journey of getting the skills, knowledge and mindset to improve the rate at which your company learns. The rest you will learn only by doing. After every chapter, practise what you learn. Gather feedback. Share it with others. Repeat these steps to learn at speed how to learn at speed.

Ready to win?

References

Brende, B (2019) We need a reskilling revolution. Here's how to make it happen, *World Economic Forum*, https://www.weforum.org/agenda/2019/04/skills-jobs-investing-in-people-inclusive-growth/ (archived at https://perma.cc/574Z-YBYL)

ETH Zurich (2020) Grasping exponential growth, *Science Daily*, 14 December, https://www.sciencedaily.com/releases/2020/12/201214090145.htm (archived at https://perma.cc/BLK6-MGDJ)

Grove, A (1995) *High Output Management,* Vintage Books, London https://www.spglobal.com/marketintelligence/en/news-insights/latest-news-headlines/us-corporate-bankruptcy-count-in-2020-nears-500-as-filings-continue-to-climb-60249430 (archived at https://perma.cc/R92C-CWRQ)

Ries, E (2011) *The Lean Startup: How constant innovation creates radically successful businesses*, Portfolio Penguin

Sweney, M and Butler, S (2021) Asos triples profits as Covid crisis boosts online sales, *Guardian*, 8 April, https://www.theguardian.com/business/2021/apr/08/asos-triples-profits-as-covid-crisis-boosts-online-sales (archived at https://perma.cc/AKX8-9ZBL)

Viguerie, SP, Calder, N and Hindo, B (2021) 2021 Corporate longevity forecast, *Innosight*, https://www.innosight.com/insight/creative-destruction/ (archived at https://perma.cc/B74H-JCCS)

PART ONE

On your mark

01

Where L&D is going wrong and how Lean can fix it

So often people are working hard at the wrong thing.
Working on the right thing is probably more important than
working hard.

CATERINA FAKE, CO-FOUNDER OF FLICKR

On a hot afternoon in October 2020, Jeffrey Katzenberg, the co-founder of DreamWorks, and the former eBay and Hewlett Packard boss Meg Whitman, assembled their employees on a video call. It wasn't for a virtual coffee break. They were about to let them know that the streaming service Quibi – short for 'quick bites' – they had launched just seven months previously would be shutting down at the end of the year (Mangalindan, 2020).

Quibi had everything a startup could dream of: nearly $2 billion in funding, a long line of Hollywood talent, a team of corporate heavy-weights, free PR, and two of the brightest minds in film and technology at the helm. So, what went wrong?

By offering a paid app where you can watch short-form videos exclusively on mobile, Quibi tried to solve a problem that didn't really exist. Not only could people already get this on platforms like YouTube, Facebook and TikTok for only the cost of their digital soul, but streaming had made standard units of time for entertainment irrelevant. Episodes could be 20 minutes or an hour long, and you could watch one or binge 10 at a time.

The short-form streaming company didn't understand that the way people consume content had changed. The younger generation didn't just want to watch stuff, they wanted to share it across social networks, but Quibi didn't launch with the ability to take screenshots or share clips of the shows. When the Covid-19 pandemic forced most of the world into the confines of their homes with the option of larger screens, Quibi failed to adapt and follow. They remained mobile-only for the most part and didn't release an app for Smart TVs until just one day before they announced they were closing up shop.

Their executives were in denial about competing with Netflix or other premium streaming services. Netflix is fighting for the control of your TV, they argued, while Quibi is all about your phone. Executives failed to acknowledge they were both competing for the viewer's attention. To get people to switch their attention away from watching Netflix, scrolling through TikTok and posting on Instagram, Quibi needed to give them a good reason. They didn't.

Quibi never really made the case to download the app, let alone to open it. There was no compelling value proposition to cause the buyer to commit and engage. The startup failed because no one at Quibi knew why it existed. They sunk a lot of time and money into building a product without testing assumptions. And when they did get feedback, they didn't iterate fast enough to solve the customer's problem. This isn't just the story of a startup failing, but a parable for where L&D is going wrong.

Why L&D is like a failing startup

Organizations spent over $350 billion on training in 2020 alone (Training Industry, 2021). That's more than the GDP of 160 countries. All this money was spent and what do we have to show for it? When McKinsey surveyed 1,500 managers, 75 per cent were dissatisfied with their company's L&D function. Other studies found that only 25 per cent of managers felt their training programmes made any kind of measurable improvement on performance. As little as 12 per cent of employees reported applying new skills learned in training to their jobs (Glaveski, 2019).

Given these numbers, it probably isn't surprising that only one out of every five people would recommend their organization's L&D opportunities, while nearly half wouldn't. L&D is like a startup that keeps investing its resources in creating products that the customer neither wants nor needs. Essentially, our product isn't solving the customer's problem, or at least not often enough. If it did, we would see higher satisfaction and measurable performance improvement. So, where is L&D going wrong?

Year after year, companies are putting money into training, often with the misconception that more 'interactive and fun' learning content would all of a sudden fix the ineffectiveness of their product. They focus on the fish, but what about the water? The other part, arguably the bigger part, is the context in which people operate before and after they 'learn'. This context is made up of many moving parts: goals, job roles, feedback, social norms, how people talk, how people approach problems, what's celebrated and what's left unsaid.

If the content changes but the context doesn't, it's unlikely that the products created by L&D can solve their customers' problems and support and sustain measurable performance improvement. The company's learning culture drives the context. The mere mention of the word 'culture' might evoke 'soft and fluffy' thoughts for sceptics, but this isn't about inspirational quotes on the wall, teatime, and self-congratulatory company blogs.

Culture is your shared everyday habits. It's about what you do, rather than what you say you do. And your learning culture is not just how your company learns but what you collectively do before and after you learn. It's the difference between being afraid to make mistakes and learning from them. Taking ownership and passing the buck. Candid, open feedback and behind-the-back criticism. Retaining great talent and churning your best. Executing innovative ideas and playing catchup to competitors. Your learning culture is the difference between winning and losing, yet many organizations get it wrong.

The three types of learning culture

The bottom line is that every company has a learning culture, but not every learning culture drives the bottom line. Most don't. To understand why, let's take a look at the three most common types of organizational learning culture.

Compliance-driven learning culture

These companies only value the bare minimum training to meet regulatory requirements to do business. It usually looks like a series of animated videos with a pass/fail test at the end of frantic clicking. When I ask someone how they learn at work and hear an anecdote about L&D getting in touch only to chase them on overdue compliance course deadlines, this is usually a telltale sign of a compliance-driven learning culture.

As long as L&D have a record to show successful course completion, they've 'done their job' in the eyes of the budget holder. There's almost no follow-up to see whether the employee can apply what they've learned. The percentage of the workforce who have completed the training is used to calculate Return On Investment (ROI) rather than its effectiveness in driving compliant behaviour.

If you're wondering whether the Head of L&D has a seat at the executive table in this type of organization, let me save you the trouble – they definitely don't. Does this sound like your organization? If yes, your business is at risk. You'll soon find yourself lagging much further behind your competition, seeing higher talent turnover and a growing reluctance to organizational change of any kind.

Process-driven learning culture

Although learning is still largely dominated by top-down mandatory training in these companies, it goes beyond the compliance tick box to deliver training that supports business processes – for example, onboarding for new starters or training to accompany the rollout of a new tool. There's a strong focus on the delivery of training rather than the actual learning. The delivery is 'sage on the stage' classroom training, one-size-fits-all, pushed out on L&D's schedule and at a time when it bears little immediate relevance to the employee, followed by a 'smiley face' feedback sheet.

The compliance-learning culture conditions employees to learn only when they've been told to; however, employees learn only when it's absolutely necessary in process-driven learning cultures. The risk is that the necessity is often defined by someone who doesn't know the business challenges or the employees' needs as well as they do. You also have to sign up for the whole curriculum, even if you only need 10 minutes' worth. It's like meal prepping for the entire week on Sunday, but being forced to eat it all on Monday.

In these companies, L&D professionals respond to every business process challenge with a course. Even managers make the same mistake when they pack their team members off on a five-day training course at the first sign of 'trouble', hoping they'll come back enlightened. There's never a question about whether there will be a course or not. Instead, it's whether this time you'll be creating one or buying a library of a gazillion courses, because the more the merrier, right? When employees don't engage with the generic courses, L&D often makes optional learning mandatory. That will do it.

The other challenge is the lack of meaningful involvement or buy-in from managers. Managers often don't always follow up after training, or even know what their employees are learning. Employees return to their 'desk' and don't get an opportunity to apply what they've learned. With no reinforcement from the manager or, even worse, pushback for trying what they've learned, people just revert to their old ways. This isn't just poor ROI; employees and managers become cynical of L&D and its ability to drive real behavioural change.

Skills-driven learning culture

Here the focus is building skills that will help individuals progress in their careers and stay at the company. Learning is valued and seen to close skills gaps, but the business will prescribe the learning for skills they want. Occasionally, you might get some informal learning resources sent via email or your internal chat. Still, upskilling remains largely event-based, with long-structured programmes that take you away from your job. The approach is like a self-fulfilling prophecy whereby you go into the course and supposedly come out 'upskilled'.

People are nominated to 'receive' learning, probably based on once-a-year development discussions. The risk is that people learn the wrong thing at the wrong time for the wrong reasons. For example, you'll find people racking up CPD points and certifications to signal they are 'ready' for a promotion. Still, the money spent on training doesn't necessarily translate into better performance or real business impact. If you've been building up vanity learning KPIs to suggest you warrant a promotion but you don't get it, you're probably now less likely to invest your time and effort into learning again.

In these companies, training still isn't personalized to the company or individual. Typically, instructional designers will buy or take months to build generic programmes that don't consider the business's unique circumstances. If an individual is at a lower or higher proficiency level for a particular skill than what the training was designed for, they end up getting more or less of what they actually need.

Aside from that, learning is not continuous and takes a long time to create, by which point the priorities of the business can change. This is often ineffective for the organization and 'busy' employees who already say they struggle to find time to learn. Although the skills-driven approach has the right intentions to align learning with business needs, it assumes that the employee is a passive spectator waiting to be entertained, rather than the co-creator of their growth.

What is Lean Learning and why does it matter?

Organizations with these three types of learning cultures struggle to keep up with the pace of change to varying degrees. They all face the challenge of gaining the knowledge and skills at the speed and frequency demanded by the current business climate – the knowledge and skills to sell and support new products with only a short time to market, continuously adopt new technologies, and mobilize talent to serve new in-demand roles.

Their learning cultures don't support the organization to learn fast enough. When the world outside the organization is changing more quickly than inside, the end is likely near. L&D needs to be better, faster and cheaper in the new world of work. But, most importantly, it needs to drive performance to be seen as a critical function in the business. In the face of exponential change, no employee has the time for training for the sake of training. Paradoxically, they require less learning to perform better.

Performance matters. It's what the business stakeholders care about. It's what the employees want to improve. It's what the learning culture should be driving. In the other learning cultures, they hire and promote based on skills but fire for performance? The logic doesn't stack up. Would you keep someone in your team who had the skills on paper but couldn't apply them to perform better? Probably not.

Yet only about 10 per cent of organizations consistently measure the impact of learning on employee performance – the rest look at survey feedback and quiz results that rarely correlate to performance improvement on the job. Whilst the other learning cultures only look at learning, performance-driven learning cultures prioritize the application of learning.

A single-minded focus on improving performance encompasses the best parts of the other types of learning cultures. It drives compliant behaviour, mastery of processes and the development of in-demand skills, because if they are all aligned to business goals, they will contribute to better performance.

It's time for a new approach

The traditional approach to workplace learning was not optimized to drive performance. Organizations need to connect the right learning resources to the right person at the right time to have the right business impact. They need to be able to do this at speed, repeatedly. This is where Lean Learning comes in. It's a radical alternative to a 'waterfall' approach, such as ADDIE (Assess, Design, Develop, Implement, Evaluate), traditionally used by L&D teams.

Lean Learning is about helping teams learn what matters in the shortest time, apply it in the moments that shape performance, and iterate based on feedback until you solve the business problem. The approach provides employees with initial learning combined with ongoing performance support, opportunities to practise, and knowledge sharing. Lean Learning cuts waste by removing any step that doesn't add value and focusing on delivering just enough learning at the point of need to drive measurable performance improvement.

Lean Learning isn't shorter courses or producing the same amount of content faster. Neither is it a new way of designing learning content or a new L&D buzzword. It's not about doing more of the same. In fact, it's a game-changer. It completely changes how we think and do organizational learning, with every aspect from defining the problem to delivering learning experiences built from the ground up with performance at the heart of it.

What next?

Lean Learning is more than a process change. It's a culture change that lets us approach our work as a learning experience, creates inclusive environments and drives us to be better. In other words, Lean Learning is how organizations learn now.

Before we dive into the steps for implementing Lean Learning, it's important to understand the foundation it's built on. In the next chapter, we'll look at the nine mindset shifts needed to enable learning at speed.

References

Glaveski, S (2019) Where companies go wrong with learning and development, *Harvard Business Review*, https://hbr.org/2019/10/where-companies-go-wrong-with-learning-and-development (archived at https://perma.cc/HN5R-EVFU)

Mangalindan, JP (2020) Quibi leaders' $1.7 billion failure is a story of self-sabotage, *Bloomberg*, 11 November, https://www.bloomberg.com/news/features/2020-11-11/what-went-wrong-at-quibi-jeffrey-katzenberg-meg-whitman-and-self-sabotage (archived at https://perma.cc/4GRH-FT7G)

Training Industry (2021) Size of the Training Industry, https://trainingindustry.com/wiki/outsourcing/size-of-training-industry/ (archived at https://perma.cc/5QEY-JAZK)

02

How to think Lean Learning before you do it

Champions behave like champions before they're champions; they have a winning standard of performance before they're winners.

BILL WALSH, AMERICAN FOOTBALL COACH

Since Satya Nadella joined Microsoft as CEO in 2014, he has transformed the company from a stagnating, siloed business into an economic juggernaut. A big part of his explanation for this turnaround: a shift in mindset. In his 2017 book, *Hit Refresh: The quest to rediscover Microsoft's soul and imagine a better future for everyone*, he describes that when he became CEO, morale was low. PC sales were declining in favour of tablets and phones. Microsoft's then-recent products had not seen major success, and its Bing search engine was not competing effectively with Google.

Many in the organization wanted to look like the smartest person in the room. People in this mindset struggle to admit their weaknesses and become defensive when their mistakes are pointed out. They take fewer risks and end up innovating less. The fixed mindset can be profoundly destructive.

Microsoft would need to change how it developed products, earned its revenues, and managed its people to overcome business challenges. This required new skills. Building on the work of Stanford psychologist Dr Carol Dweck, Nadella worked to shift thinking from a 'fixed mindset' culture to a 'growth mindset' (Dweck, 2012). A growth mindset believes that talent should be developed in everyone, not viewed as a fixed, innate gift that some have, and others don't.

Joe Whittinghill, Corporate Vice President of Talent, Learning and Insights at Microsoft, said the tech giant instilled growth mindset at scale by helping employees and managers understand what a growth mindset is and how to apply it. They empowered managers and employees with the methods to shift the mindset, drive behaviour change and get results. To become an organization of 'learn-it-alls'. The result? Microsoft stock soared 90 per cent, from $90 to almost $175 – nearly three times more than where Bill Gates left it when he handed the CEO slot to Steve Ballmer in January 2000.

The Microsoft turnaround is an excellent example of the power of a mindset shift. If Nadella had tried to make strategic changes in the organization without shifting the mindset, there would have been too much inertia to battle. Mindset influences behaviour, behaviour drives results, and results reaffirm our mindset. Before you can *do* Lean Learning, you need to *think* Lean Learning. Only when our organization shifts mindset can it embed Lean Learning in its cultural DNA and radically improve its capability of driving performance with learning at speed.

The Lean Learning mindset

In the rest of this chapter, we'll look at the mindset shifts required to practise Lean Learning. The expectation is not for you to transform your thinking by the end of the chapter but to understand the principles that guide the Lean Learning process.

Think of Lean Learning as a recipe and the mindset shifts as the ingredients. As with recipes, if you don't understand why you need each step, you'll start to skip steps. Once you're aware of the mindsets, you'll understand why each step in the Lean Learning process exists as you progress through the book.

Mindset shift #1: Love the problem

Your L&D strategy must solve a problem for the employee and organization. To do that, you must love the problem. Why should you love it? Because your solution can only be as good as your understanding of the problem.

As Albert Einstein is believed to have once said, 'If I only had one hour to solve a problem, I'd spend 55 minutes defining the problem, and the remaining five solving it.' When you jump to a solution without deeply understanding the problem, there's a higher risk of investing time and resources into something that might address symptoms of the pain but not the root cause.

When we fall in love with our solution instead of the problem, we sink resources into a training programme that sucks up a lot of time from employees but then adds no value. Our love for the solution can make us do crazy things. For example, instead of designing a solution for the problem, we can find ourselves trying to make the problem fit into the solution.

Have you ever purchased enterprise-wide licences for a course library and then tried to find a course from it to solve every business problem? Your view of the problem is skewed by the solution you want to implement, so you lose focus on the actual business challenge and your internal customers' needs. When you're attached to the solution, and it fails, the project stops. When you fall in love with the problem, and the solution fails, you circle back to the problem and try again. For example, let's look at why Blockbuster isn't Netflix.

Blockbuster had the rental history of all of their customers, data on where they lived, and even their payment details on file. They knew video streaming was coming, but they were too attached to their current solution. Blockbuster's biggest revenue generators were late fees and the sale of in-store concessions. In the face of technological change, they were too focused on trying to optimize for the present to move the company towards streaming. Blockbuster was essentially stuck at the local maximum rather than the global maximum (Hastings, 2020). This is a common pitfall incumbent businesses find themselves in. The local maximum represents a solution that delivers more value than previous iterations but is not the best possible solution for the problem.

By focusing on the local maximum, organizations miss the opportunity to move to the global maximum. On the other hand, Netflix focused on the problem and moved from local maximum to global maximum by pivoting the business from mailing DVDs to customers to the leading streaming service.

When you focus on the problem, it opens up a whole world of solutions. You can test and see which one solves the problem best. But when you focus on a single solution, you have many unsolved problems. In Chapter 3, we'll look at how you can better find, define, and understand problems.

Mindset shift #2: Bias towards action

For an organization to keep up and thrive in the era of exponential change, L&D teams must prioritize speed of execution over perfect execution. When we take too long to act, we're at the risk of the situation changing, making any action we later take irrelevant for the employees' present needs. Actions and results speak louder than beautiful courses and carefully crafted strategies when the pace of change is only getting faster.

Bias for action accelerates learning that can help improve your results. Suppose we try out a solution – taking that action will uncover the parameters of the problem and the limitations and capabilities of our resources. The action generates new knowledge that informs the next action. The more types of action we take, the faster we learn what works and what doesn't.

We won't become a great footballer watching Lionel Messi play. We won't become incredible singers listening to Adele albums. We won't become fluent in speaking French by just thinking about it all day. We learn by doing. That applies to learning what learning will drive a measurable performance improvement. We only get better at it when we do it. Again and again.

The sooner we connect our learning experience with our target audience, the sooner we can get feedback and incorporate it into the next iteration. The shorter the iterations, the faster we learn, and our people will learn. Our learning about what drives performance compounds improving our ability to drive performance with every action.

When you have a bias for action, you will avoid excessive approval workflows and spending too much time planning because it delays the opportunity to get feedback and increases the likelihood of missing the window of need. A bias for action will also enable you to be quick and clear to communicate a problem and directly ask leaders for a decision instead of dancing around the issue.

We won't be afraid to make decisions when the going gets tough, and even when it's not our job, we won't hesitate to roll up our sleeves and get the work done. The mindset creates an openness to leverage the skills of others to get things done and involve our internal customers in the process. When we act and get things done, it motivates others to take the initiative too.

On the other hand, a bias for action does not mean acting impulsively. Taking risks without considering consequences isn't a smart move in your personal life or for your company. It's important to find the earliest point where you have enough information to take action.

For example, social media scheduling startup Buffer created a landing page in hours to test the demand for their product that was yet to be built. This experiment gave Buffer positive feedback and information about the customer's need to take the next action without wasting much time and money (Gascoigne, 2011).

Imagine if they had waited to build the entire product before getting their first feedback, only to find out they didn't have the features people needed. They would have delayed the opportunity to learn and wasted resources unnecessarily. By finding an earlier point to take the right action, Buffer could reduce the risk and learn faster. In Part Three, we'll look at how L&D teams can use Minimum Valuable Learning to act faster and get feedback quicker.

To shift our mindset to have a bias towards action, we first need to change our perception of risk. We often associate taking the wrong action with risk but overlook the risk of inaction. What about the risk of not learning what doesn't work faster? What if the risk of doing nothing is missing the opportunity to jump from a shallow linear curve to an accelerating trajectory of performance improvement? That would change our notion of risk.

We also need to remove the friction in the decision-making process. If you currently have many people who could say no, while no one can clearly say go, this environment is counterproductive for enabling learning at speed. When L&D need to get approval from stakeholder after stakeholder just to test an idea, it can curb the momentum and desire to take action. The autonomy to try new things without too many hoops to jump through is critical for teams to take action.

If the standard decision-making process in your organization is months of meetings and presentations to committees, the concept of acting quickly without a 'perfect' plan can be unsettling. To overcome this, your team must build a habit of being decisive, recognizing that no amount of information gathering, expertise, or having the right circumstance will lead you to the one true answer because it doesn't exist. At some point, you have to move forward with what you have.

Mindset shift #3: Fail fast, fail often

When we fear failure, it inhibits us from experimenting and taking risks. The mindset restricts the ability of organizations and teams to innovate and improve. If companies are not prepared to fail, they're not prepared to learn. Ultimately, these organizations will not learn fast enough and will be beaten by competitors. Ironically, trying to avoid failure increases the likelihood of it happening in more glorious ways.

To succeed, organizations must be open to failure, but this is just the first step. The intention is to ensure we keep learning from our mistakes and failures and use that to move close to our target. Iterating fast failures achieves the desired result faster than perfecting a solution. A fail-fast mindset is about testing the trickiest assumptions as quickly as possible and using failure as a learning experience to move close to your target. The faster you fail, the faster you will get to that next version.

When we don't have this mindset, we spend a lot of time and money only to find out our ideas don't work. Then, we spend even more time dwelling on the failure, wondering why it happened or blaming others. There is no time for that if you want to learn at speed. We must be able to test ideas quickly, and when they don't work, we should be able to bounce back up to our feet almost before we hit the ground.

The 'fail fast, fail often' mindset empowers people to develop a large pipeline of ideas and options, making the business more resilient to change. In the face of uncertainty, it enables teams to experiment with confidence. Companies can change more rapidly by trying new things quickly with more openness to experimentation. Amazon CEO Jeff Bezos believes failed experiments are a necessary evil for creating successful inventions (Kim, 2016).

Amazon has shut down countless failed projects over the past two decades. For example, the hotel booking site Amazon Destination, its auctions site Amazon Auctions, and their first smartphone, Fire Phone. But the billions of dollars of failure has not stopped Amazon from continuing to experiment.

According to Bezos, 'If you decide that you're going to do only the things you know are going to work, you're going to leave a lot of opportunity on the table.' Some of Amazon's largest businesses, such as Amazon Web Services and Prime, are bets that paid off.

This mindset shift allows teams to entertain creative ideas that would be too risky with a fail-big fail-last approach. The mindset builds a culture of iterative innovation, zeal to learn, and skill enhancement in the organization. It also drastically reduces the time taken to solve the problem for the customer.

Amazon Web Services, for example, was first to market with a modern cloud infrastructure service, and it took several years before a competitor responded. As such, they currently control a vast amount of market share.

Whether you're an employee or an organization, there is no learning without failing. L&D play an instrumental role in creating a culture where employees can try new things, make mistakes and learn from them without the fear of damaging their reputation or career.

Failing fast is a critical aspect of the Lean Learning process. Much like any scientific process, the quickest way to disprove a hypothesis is for an experiment that tests that hypothesis to fail to give the expected result.

Openness toward failure is crucial to make it a productive occurrence, and this requires leaders to lead by example in regard to risk-taking. This way, employees can understand that this is a practice that is not shunned and that they can benefit from undertaking it. By shifting from 'Who allowed this to happen?' to 'What can we learn from this and how could we have learned it earlier?' we value the learning and development from the experience as much as the result.

Without a 'fail fast, fail often' approach, you'll end up in a situation where you've spent months 'perfecting' something, only to find out it doesn't work. Instead, you could test in weeks and learn from what didn't work to improve it. But with this mindset shift, you are never failing.

As long as you keep learning from your mistakes and failures, you succeed by moving closer to your target. In Part Three of this book, we'll look at methods that put this mindset into play and how they help your organization enable learning at speed.

Mindset shift #4: Continuous improvement

Continuous improvement is the cornerstone of Lean and Agile methodologies. But it isn't something you do once, and then it's done. Continuous improvement is a deliberate decision to invest in and focus on getting better continuously. It's an ongoing way of operating.

Continuous improvement, or Kaizen, was developed to improve Japanese manufacturing processes by lowering costs and improving quality. Kaizen translates to 'change for better', a simple concept that companies now use all over the world at individual, team and organizational levels (Imai, 1986).

When everyone in the organization is in a permanent state of 'work in progress', they will be open to learning from mistakes, each other, and experiences. What you know becomes less relevant than what you may learn, and knowing the answer to questions becomes less critical than having the ability to ask the right questions in the first place.

The very existence of L&D is an acknowledgement that company operations can always be better than they were yesterday. We should constantly look for ways to improve how we operate to achieve our desired outcome. This mindset helps you avoid the trap of becoming too anchored in your current thinking. It overcomes the inertia of sticking to existing solutions even when they're sub-optimal. It also recognizes that there is always new information to be learned – it creates openness and a pathway to incorporating further information into our current point of view.

Continuous improvement helps cut down the upfront resource requirements, reduce waste, and accelerate value creation time. Every failure and setback on a work in progress is immediate feedback of what's working and what's not, which helps you get better. This approach ensures you use your fast failures as a learning experience to get to the next version of your learning strategy. Failure is a part of the continuous improvement process.

Constant feedback is an essential aspect of continuous improvement. Some of the most successful startups often release their product, even though imperfect, for beta testing to improve quickly. Gmail, for example, launched in 2004 but only left official beta in 2009, even though millions of people were already using it (Lapidos, 2009). Similarly, employee feedback is necessary for enabling performance-driven learning. In Part Three, we'll look at methods L&D can use to start gathering feedback from internal customers as early as possible and continually improve their learning strategy at a faster pace.

A problem-first approach also helps drive continuous improvement. A course is not 'done' once we push it out to employees. Instead, we must get feedback and improve on it until it solves the problem. Sometimes those improvements are big; often, they are small. But what's most important is that they're frequent.

It's also important to measure where you started and where you have arrived to show that you really have made improvements. In Chapter 8, we'll look at how you can generate proof of impact that helps you effectively track continuous improvement.

Being always a 'work in progress' is a lifelong commitment to continuous improvement. It's the commitment organizations, individuals and L&D need to make to excel in the face of unstoppable, ever-present change.

Mindset shift #5: Riskiest assumptions first

Where would you start if you had to teach a monkey to recite Shakespeare on a pedestal? Astro Teller, the 'captain of moonshots' at Google's innovation lab X, suggests many people tend to rush off and start building the pedestal just to have a sense of progress and to have at least something to show their boss. However, according to Teller (2016), the right answer is training the monkey.

This is because training a monkey is infinitely harder than building a pedestal. It would be a waste if you find out it's impossible to train the monkey after spending time and money building a pedestal. All of the risk and the learning comes from the difficult task of training the monkey, so it's imperative to do the harder thing first.

In *The Lean Startup*, the term 'Leap of Faith' describes the riskiest assumptions for your product or service (Ries, 2011). When you front-load the work that will lead to the greatest learning rate, you de-risk the riskiest parts of your endeavour first. This approach not only reduces the chance of you going belly up, but if it does go wrong, at least you learned before you sank any further time and resources.

When implementing a learning strategy, L&D teams often start by thinking about what courses we need, how we will be creating these, and how we will know people have done them. These assumptions represent the pedestal. The riskier assumptions are whether we're solving the right problem, whether our solution will drive the desired behaviour change, and how we will know whether that change has solved our problem. This is our monkey.

For example, you might spend a lot of money shooting a high-production-value training video, but what if the substance in the video doesn't actually help solve the business challenge? To tackle the riskiest assumption first, you could shoot a video on your phone with the same substance to see if it drives the expected behaviour change first before you look to embellish with production values.

In an attempt to show progress, L&D often rush to create and procure things rather than spending more time upfront on validating the riskiest assumptions. As a result, we only get to the difficult stuff when our excitement and energy have run out. We only come to find out the strategy's viability after sinking lots of time and resources into it.

Tackling the hardest assumptions first forces us to ask better questions, which can lead to vastly different approaches. Some of these will be blind alleys that lead to nowhere, but others will be game-changers that can transform business performance.

Mindset shift #6: You get what you measure

If you use a health app or fitness tracker, you've probably checked your step count at least once today. Suppose you've not hit your target of 10,000 steps, then you're likely to consider taking a little walk. Why? What we measure affects what we do. If you weigh yourself once a week, you will probably eat more salads and less fast food at lunchtime. Record on the fridge who's done the chores this week, and it will bring a focus to the person who hasn't; the measurement is enough to drive change.

If we measure the wrong thing, we will do the wrong thing. If we don't measure something, it becomes neglected, as if the problems didn't exist. This maxim is as true for individuals as it is for businesses. Every metric, whether used explicitly to influence behaviour, evaluate future strategies, or simply take stock, will affect actions and decisions.

Imagine an organization that measures time spent learning rather than performance improvement (this probably won't require much imagination). In this organization, the L&D team and managers begin to pay more attention to the amount of time people spend learning. Once people start spending more time learning, the L&D team and managers get rewarded with bonuses and even promotions. Consequently, this drives them to take further decisions and actions to improve the time spent learning metric.

Over time the L&D team and managers become stronger at increasing time spent learning. But what if a high time spent learning didn't lead to better business performance? Even worse, what if it leads to counterproductive decisions and actions? For example, in an attempt to rack up the hours, employees are distracted from doing their work, which negatively affects their performance. The organization becomes what it measures, and what we measure is all we get.

Whether you're a newly formed startup or a global enterprise, the path to success is dependent on making critical decisions along the way. Organizations use data to choose strategies and allocate resources. The right metric can determine how L&D is prioritized in the business. Let's say L&D teams could show data that demonstrated a high course completion rate or data that showed an increase in sales due to learning. Which one do you think will get L&D more buy-in from the leadership?

While both data points can be helpful, the latter alone demonstrates value. L&D teams often stop at the point of tracking activity data such as completion rates and time spent learning. So, even if they had improved business performance, they wouldn't be able to show it because they never measured the appropriate data in the first place. In other words, what we measure limits what the business believes we can achieve.

Mindset shift #7: Outcome over outputs

It can often feel like there is lots to do and not enough time and resources to do it. Keeping our focus might feel like an unattainable goal with so many tasks fighting for our attention. However, to ensure we focus on the tasks that matter, we need to prioritize outcome over output. Let's first look at the difference between the two.

Outputs are what we build. They're the courses we author, the workshops we host and the technology we buy. On the other hand, outcomes are the impact we make due to our outputs. The business challenges we solve and the behaviour we change. The outcome is output plus value. Without the value, you can create as much output as possible, but it doesn't equal success. Output without the value is essentially waste.

An outcome-first mindset shapes how L&D perceive success. For example, if you're output-focused, you probably consider the number of learning programmes you launched as a measure of success. However, if you're outcome-focused, you would use impact on business performance to measure success. L&D teams that manage projects in terms of outputs rather than outcomes often settle for 'done' rather than doing the hard work of targeting measurable performance improvement.

The goal of the L&D team (or any team for that matter) is not to produce outputs; it's to reach a specific outcome. A successful team seeks to maximize outcomes with minimal output. That way, you get as close to the desired change in the organization with the least amount of initial and ongoing work as possible.

Without this mindset shift, you can spend time producing lots of courses rather than curating the content that solves the problem today. You can end up tracking how many people completed the course rather than how many people improved their performance as a result. You can get fixated on getting things 'done' rather than doing things that drive success.

When we focus on outcomes, we don't spend time working on things that don't produce the desired results. We remain focused on solving the problem and adding value to the individual and organization. The outcome mindset ensures we measure the right metric and keep iterating until we see the progress towards our target. It encourages us to fail fast, get feedback and continuously improve our solution.

When we're working to deliver the scope of the outcome rather than a specific output, it gives us the flexibility to change our strategy as we learn more about the problem and possible solutions. Traditionally, L&D teams have worked to deliver on the scope of output which they defined when they first started the project and were at the maximum point of ignorance about the problem and possible solution. This approach can also pressure you to deliver all the requirements in the output scope, even if you know it's unnecessary or won't add any value.

When we prioritize outcomes over output, it forces us to make challenging decisions. You might have to scrap weeks of work if it's not moving you closer to the desired outcome. The sunk costs might feel like a waste, but learning what doesn't work is invaluable. The real waste is continuing to invest time and money in something that doesn't work for the sake of delivering an output when you could be focusing on something that might actually work.

Mindset shift #8: Eliminate waste

In traditional project management practices like Waterfall, we're forced to predict all the aspects of a solution right at the beginning, when we know the least. With this approach, we rarely adapt significantly in the face of new evidence or learning. Too much effort has already been sunk upfront, resulting in output absorbing resources but not adding value. This is a waste.

Software development has a similar issue when Waterfall is used rather than Agile, with waste coming from predicting what features the users want based on a whole load of assumptions. A 2019 report from Pendo found that 80 per cent of features are rarely or never used in the average cloud software product. Pendo estimates that these unused features represent $29.5 billion in R&D investment by publicly traded cloud companies (Pendo, 2019).

As we saw in the previous chapter, L&D in many organizations tells a very similar story, with evidence showing a lack of meaningful impact compared to the extraordinary amount of money that has been spent. The L&D wasteland is littered with unused licences to content libraries, training days that were a 'fun' day out of the office, and learning management systems that everyone complains about.

Organizations need to cut the waste to enable learning at speed. To achieve this, L&D must focus on eliminating anything that does not add value. In Toyota's school of Lean manufacturing, waste (or muda) is categorized into seven types: over-production, unnecessary transportation, motion, inventory, waiting, defects, and over-processing (Womack and Jones, 2003).

Here are the types of waste adapted for L&D:

- **Over-production:** Creating content when it is not needed or could be curated faster.

- **Unnecessary content and tools:** Pushing lots of irrelevant content and tools frustrates the internal customer and takes up too much administrative effort.

- **Delays in the process:** Bureaucracy and approval steps delay how quickly you can deliver something to employees and slow down the feedback loops.

- **Lack of measurement:** Tracking vanity metrics or not tracking data at all results in work that adds no value, low stakeholder buy-in, and slows down feedback loops.

- **Undefined problem:** A problem that's not clearly defined results in a lack of focus and delays time to solve the problem for internal customers.

- **Poor communication:** Friction in communication results in delays, confusion, and damages perception of L&D.

- **Non-utilized talent:** Not tapping into the skills and knowledge of internal experts to enable learning across the organization.

Mindset shift #9: Empower the team

Teams are empowered when they have more autonomy to think, behave, act, react and control their work. Why is this so important? Because empowered teams can truly serve the internal customer rather than simply serving 'the leadership'. When L&D teams are empowered, they are more likely to implement learning strategies that meet the rapidly changing needs of their customer than if they were taking orders from people who might not be familiar with the details of the problem.

Employee empowerment is often misunderstood as taking your hands off to let employees sink or swim. That's neglect, not empowerment. Empowerment is an active, ongoing process. It involves coaching or teaching team members to self-serve, become adaptive, make decisions, and make them right without needing instructions or approval.

Employees don't suddenly feel empowered because managers tell them they are or because companies issue statements saying it is part of the culture. It's about changing how you work, providing the tools and resources, encouragement and motivation to create and sustain empowerment.

Empowerment starts with leaders leaning in to enable employees. For example, rather than leaders prescribing the solution, they should guide the L&D team to define and shape the problem, then let them develop the solution. This enables the team to keep iterating until they solve the problem, rather than coming back to the leader when they've implemented the suggested solution when it doesn't work.

L&D leaders can empower their own team by opening up the extent to which they can make decisions without approval. By clearly communicating goals, we can help team members develop their own plans to achieve them and build up team confidence by discovering their own solutions and answers instead of telling them how to do things.

On the other hand, L&D teams can empower managers to nurture their teams' growth. The manager intimately understands the business challenges and pain points, so they can help solve those challenges with learning when empowered. L&D teams can also empower employees to own their development. Instead of micromanaging employee learning, L&D should make employees aware of business challenges and desired outcomes and trust they will learn what they need.

When you help employees understand why their learning will contribute to their own improvement and the organization's performance, they're more likely to act than if you told them they have to do it because they've been told to. Empowered employees know how their learning and development can make a difference to the organization and why it is significant. In Chapters 5–7, we'll go into different tactics you can use to empower employees to become autonomous learners.

What next?

Your mindset shapes how you make sense of the world and yourself. It influences how you think, feel and behave in any given situation. Thinking Lean Learning is the first step to doing it.

In Part Two, we'll begin to go through the steps of the Lean Learning process. Use the mindsets covered in this chapter as a reference to remind yourself why each step matters. If you face hurdles as you try to implement the steps, think about how you can help your peers and stakeholders to embrace the relevant mindset.

References

Dweck, C (2012) *Mindset: How you can fulfil your potential*, Robinson

Gascoigne, J (2011) Idea to paying customers in 7 weeks: How we did it, *Buffer* [Blog], 16 February, https://buffer.com/resources/idea-to-paying-customers-in-7-weeks-how-we-did-it/ (archived at https://perma.cc/8DXA-HEJH)

Hastings, R (2020) CEO Reed Hastings on how Netflix beat Blockbuster, *Marketplace*, 8 September, https://www.marketplace.org/2020/09/08/ceo-reed-hastings-on-how-netflix-beat-blockbuster/ (archived at https://perma.cc/73EE-BEG7)

Imai, M (1986) *Kaizen: The key to Japan's competitive success*, McGraw Hill

Kim, E (2016) How Amazon CEO Jeff Bezos has inspired people to change the way they think about failure, *Business Insider*, 28 May, https://www.businessinsider.com/how-amazon-ceo-jeff-bezos-thinks-about-failure-2016-5 (archived at https://perma.cc/2QG5-FGCB)

Lapidos, J (2009) Why did it take Google so long to take Gmail out of 'beta'?, *Slate*, 7 July, https://slate.com/news-and-politics/2009/07/why-google-kept-gmail-in-beta-for-so-many-years.html (archived at https://perma.cc/CB5S-CG7U)

Nadella, S (2017) *Hit Refresh: The quest to rediscover Microsoft's soul and imagine a better future for everyone*, Harper Business

Pendo (2019) The 2019 Feature Adoption Report, https://www.pendo.io/resources/the-2019-feature-adoption-report/ (archived at https://perma.cc/8RMV-R2FX)

Ries, E (2011) *The Lean Startup: How today's entrepreneurs use continuous innovation to create radically successful businesses*, Currency

Teller, A (2016) Tackle the monkey first, *X Company* [Blog], 7 December, https://blog.x.company/tackle-the-monkey-first-90fd6223e04d (archived at https://perma.cc/W76D-8HLQ)

Walsh, B (2010) *Score Takes Care Of Itself: My philosophy of leadership*, Portfolio

Womack, JP and Jones, DT (2003) *Lean Thinking: Banish waste and create wealth in your corporation*, Simon and Schuster

PART TWO

Get set

03

Find the right business problem to solve

The value of a company is the sum of the problems you solve together.

MARTIN LORENTZON, CO-FOUNDER OF SPOTIFY

Michael Dubin found himself at a Christmas party talking to one of his father's friends. The conversation took an unexpected turn, and before long, Dubin had offered to help him offload a surplus supply of razors from a previous failed business venture (we've all been there, right?). However, this wasn't just a favour. Dubin saw it as an opportunity to address his frustrations with 'overpriced' razor blades and the 'cumbersome' buying experience in stores by creating a direct-to-home razor subscription service. Dollar Shave Club (DSC) was born (Ransom, 2021).

Fast forward five years, DSC was acquired for $1 billion by Unilever. How did they grow so fast with such a simple solution in a competitive industry with giants like Gillette? They did many things right, like their infamous viral video packed with unexpected twists – a toddler shaving a man's head, a giant bear, a machete to cut packing tape. But most importantly, they were able to identify and address an actual problem in the industry. And they persuaded consumers, who were finally hearing what they had been thinking all along.

Finding the right problem to solve is as crucial for building a successful startup as it is for building a learning strategy. The problem you're trying to solve is the attribute of workplace learning that motivates employees to learn, and it's what aligns L&D and the business on what matters the most. It's your North Star. Like its namesake Polaris in the sky, you use it to navigate your learning strategy in the right direction.

Without a rigorous approach to finding the right problem, organizations will miss opportunities, waste resources and end up pursuing learning initiatives that aren't aligned with business goals. Answering 'are we learning the right things?' and 'is it working?' would make this much simpler. In this chapter, you'll discover how to find the problems in your organization to solve.

Are you solving the right problem?

Meet Melinda, Head of People Development at FiveADay.com, the global leader in supplying fruit to office workers – a fictional company I just created to illustrate how most L&D teams currently approach identifying business problems. One day Melinda gets asked by Barny, the Head of Sales, whether they can get some 'sales training'. When Melinda asks why, Barny replies that some people are not hitting targets, so he thinks a bit of training will fix them. With that, Melinda gets to work.

After a quick search on Google for sales training providers, a few posts on LinkedIn asking for recommendations, and a couple of months of running a Request For Proposal (RFP) process, Melinda finds a sales training provider that fits the budget and says they'll do the job. They bring in the trainer for a two-day course with the finest sandwiches from Denny's Cafe down the road. At which point, Melinda makes a note to herself that she probably needs a learning management system (LMS) at some point for tracking these training catering costs because you know that's a pretty big need.

A few feedback forms and months later, Melinda reports on how many people completed the training course. Did it solve the problem?

Well, if the problem is that the Head of Sales wants Sales Training, then of course. Did it solve a business problem? Probably not. This story is, unfortunately, a common occurrence in organizations where L&D are order takers rather than problem solvers.

Much like entrepreneurs in love with their solution even before they've validated whether the problem exists, many L&D teams often start suggesting courses and training providers even before validating the problem that needs to be solved. They often rush towards a solution, fearing that if they spend too much time defining and understanding the problem, their bosses will punish them for taking too long to get started.

Ironically, you need to go slow to go fast. By putting in the time and effort required to understand the problem upfront, you increase the probability of success and avoid wasting time and money. Anyone can push training courses. Not everyone can build a learning strategy that solves a real problem for the business. That requires an incredibly deep understanding of the problem, the customer and their motivations. The Jobs-To-Be-Done framework (JTBD) has helped companies do just that for over three decades.

What are jobs to be done?

Great products start with real problems. So does great workplace learning. According to Clayton M Christensen, one of the top experts on disruptive innovation and the author of *The Innovator's Dilemma* (2013), when we buy a product or service, we essentially 'hire' it to help us do a job. The job is the goal we're trying to accomplish or the problem we're trying to resolve. If it does the job well, we'll hire it again. If it does a bad job, we 'fire' it and look for something else to solve the problem.

Harvard Business School marketing professor Theodore Levitt is attributed to have said, 'People don't want to buy a quarter-inch drill. They want a quarter-inch hole!' Similarly, we can use JTBD to explain the boom of Zoom triggered by the Covid-19 pandemic (Haider and Rasay, 2021). With many people having to work from home, the job to be done is helping remote workers manage and communicate with colleagues without in-person interaction. Zoom has seemingly done the job it was hired to do well, given that four months after the global pandemic was declared, their customers had grown by over 350 per cent.

So how do you apply the JTBD to workplace learning?

Focus on the job to be done, not the learner

The job to be done drives the product/service you hire rather than the customer. For example, if you want to collect a digital scrapbook of ideas, you can hire Pinterest. If you want to share your writing with the world, you can hire Medium. And if you want to find a date, you can hire Tinder. The users of these products are not limited to a single customer persona. In the same way, the desired outcome of the business is more important than the demographics of the employees themselves.

By mapping the learning strategy to the jobs to be done rather than job titles or departments, you can deliver learning experiences that solve the problem for everyone affected. Otherwise, resources could be wasted on generic learning programmes that don't comprehensively solve the problem for anyone. Or worse, leave out others who face the problem because they didn't fit the targeted employee profile.

Learning experiences are not the job; they're the product

The job to be done is progress you want to make in a particular circumstance rather than the learning experience. It takes you from how things are today to how you want things to be. This approach differs from organizations that deliver and track training programmes as if their mere completion is the desired outcome. The learning experience is the product hired by the business and employees to accomplish their goal or solve their problem. Completing the learning experience doesn't mean the job is done, but the right learning experience can help get the job done.

For example, Melinda (our L&D leader from FiveADay.com) might find that the worst customer interactions are due to insufficient product knowledge. So the job to be done here is delivering informative customer experiences. In this case, the 'product' the business can hire is a learning experience about product knowledge. Salespeople, support staff and the customer success team can all hire the same learning experience to get the job done. With the JTBD approach, you can personalize the product – your learning experience – to solve the problem effectively.

There are many ways to get the job done

JTBD helps you understand the alternative products a user can hire to get the same job done. For example, video conferencing and business class flights can be hired for the same job to be done – business meetings. Entrepreneurs can often fall in love with their solution and believe it's the only or best way of solving the problem. That's a risky approach as they could be oblivious that they are unsuccessful at the job their product has been hired to do by the customer. Instead, they should develop the best product to get the job done and iterate until then.

L&D professionals are not that different to founders obsessed with their products. Courses become the default response to every business challenge, but they're not the right product for the job to be done in most cases. For example, if the job is handling objections from potential customers, the employee might hire a learning resource about the most effective objection responses. That could be a course, blog, podcast, asking a colleague, or all of the above. In Chapter 5, we'll discuss all the different types of learning resources you could 'hire' to get the job done.

The JTBD approach helps you reframe the problem and understand what the learning experience needs to achieve. It gives you a way of measuring if it is working and solving the problem. But how do we find the jobs to be done?

How to find the jobs to be done

Your learning strategy starts with an idea or intuition. These are essentially 'gut feelings', but we can make them sound more scientific by calling them hypotheses. For example, imagine your employee NPS is low, and people have fed back that they're not happy about their growth opportunities. Based on this information, you might hypothesize that the problem is poor one-to-ones by managers and that it can be solved by upskilling the managers on having better career conversations.

But what if that isn't the job to be done? Even if it is, how do you know the solution you're thinking of can solve this problem? Speeding to execute a learning strategy based on incorrect assumptions is quite simply a waste of resources. The best way to avoid building something no one needs or wants is by talking to your customers. The people who you assume will hire your product to get the job done. This is where the customer discovery approach comes to play.

The customer discovery process

In his book, *The Four Steps to Epiphany*, serial entrepreneur Steve Blank originally pioneered the customer discovery process based on the steps he saw many startups take to launch successful products (Blank, 2020). It is a process that helps you validate your assumptions, put evidence behind your hypotheses, and identify the real problem that needs solving. If you want to discover the actual jobs to be done and develop a solution that solves the problem, Steve Blank explains, you need to get out of the building and interview your customers.

Customer discovery interviews are an opportunity for you to learn about the problem, not pitch a solution. The interviews will help you build a solution based on answers rather than assumptions. Fact rather than fiction. Sounds obvious, right? But most L&D teams tend only to carry out an interview (and that in the form of a survey) to get feedback on a learning event after they've sunk the time and resources. By which point, you may have already wasted effort trying to solve the wrong problem, and you could have avoided that by just speaking to employees first.

Who should I be talking to?

You have a hypothesis about the problem. You need to talk to the people in the organization who you believe are affected by this problem the most. They typically fall under three categories:

1 **Job Executor.** These are the people who would hire your product to get the job done. For example, if the job to be done is managers having better career conversations, the job executor is the manager. They are your learners. They would help you understand the underlying need and context of the problem.

2 **Job Beneficiary.** These are the people who benefit from the job to be done, but they're not involved in getting the job done. They are the employees benefiting from better career conversations carried out by the managers. The beneficiaries can help you understand the desired outcome better.

3 **Job Sponsor.** These are the people who would pay to get this job done better. For example, if the job is to respond to customer support queries faster, the Head of Customer Support would probably be the sponsor. They would help you understand what good ROI would look like for the business.

Be very specific with the customer segment you interview because the broader you go, the harder it becomes to spot patterns and draw significant insights. For example, if your job executors are managers, you might focus on managers of the same seniority level or in the same functional area. With focused targeting, 10–15 interviews can shed more meaningful insights than 50 interviews with a very broad customer segment.

How do I find people to interview?

People commonly make the mistake of reaching out to people they already know at work because it's in their comfort zone. The focus should be to reach out to people closest to the problem, and if you happen to know them well already, that's a bonus. But depending on the size of your organization, it's quite possible that you don't know everyone you need to interview personally. Don't let this hold you back.

A customer discovery interview is an opportunity to step out of your comfort zone, build cross-functional relationships and expand your network. The first reaction I get when I suggest this to L&D teams is often, 'people are too busy to make time for an interview'. The misconception is that it's hard enough to get people to training events, let alone give up their time for an interview. This is often just an assumption because they've not asked people for an interview before.

Most people you'll find are happy to help and share feedback. People like talking about themselves and the work they do. You just need to make it easy to do so, and here's how:

1 **Tell them why.** When you get in touch, clearly explain who you are and why you're asking them. It sounds like common sense; I wish it were:

   'Hey, my name is Melinda, and I'm the L&D Manager. I'm interested in supporting the sales team, and given your experience, I was hoping I could talk to you about _____.'

2 **Set the expectations.** Make sure you let people know how long the interview will take. You can do a customer interview in 15 minutes, but I recommend taking 30 minutes so you get time to build rapport:

   'I'd like to get 30 minutes of your time to learn how you _____ and get feedback on how we might be able to help.'

3 **Give your availability.** Make the process of booking a call incredibly easy for your interviewees. Cut out the back and forth of 'what time works for you?' and give them a few time options or send them a Doodle/Calendly link:

   'Do any of the times below work for you?

   Tuesday 27th June at 11 am GMT

   Wednesday 28th June at 2 pm GMT

Thursday 29th June at 9 am GMT

If none of the above work, please feel free to let me know a few dates/times that would work for you. The only day I can't do is Fridays.'

4 **Confirm how to connect.** If you're based in the same building or close enough to meet in person, I recommend an in-real-life (IRL) meetup in an informal location. Coffee shops work great. Alternatively, you can do it only over a video call. Whatever you decide, make sure to communicate it:

'We can meet at the Denny's Cafe [Add link], 2 minutes from the office. Coffee's on me.'

What questions should I ask in the interview?

When someone decides whether to hire a product to get a job done, they find themselves in the middle of four forces that influence their motivation to change. Push and pull are forces that drive progress, whilst anxiety and habits are forces that keep the status quo. When push and pull are greater than anxiety and habit, you get behaviour change. If not, then the problem you're trying to solve isn't worth the perceived pain of change.

The customer discovery interview is about getting the customer to talk about their workflow and underlying motivations so you can understand the forces at play. The right questions combined with a healthy dose of curiosity can yield brilliant insights that help you build a solution that solves the right problem. Let's take a look at each force and examples of questions you can use to identify it.

1. PUSH

Push is everything about your current situation that you're unhappy with. The trigger that prompts you to search for something better. These could be:

- **External pushes:** You didn't hit the sales target, received negative customer feedback, or had continuously delayed product releases.

- **Internal pushes:** You don't feel confident about client interactions or feel like you're falling behind on the latest technologies.

Here are examples of questions to help you identify the push force:

- What event or feeling prompted you to want to solve the problem?
- When has this problem come up before, and how did you deal with it then?
- Why are you not happy with the current situation?
- Why does solving this problem matter to you?
- What would happen if you didn't solve this problem in the next month? Three months?

2. PULL

Pull is the attraction towards the promised land. What is the desired outcome? What does the person consider to be progress? This could be:

- **The idea of a better life:** You think learning something will make you more productive or a better leader.
- **A pull toward a particular solution:** If you were on a call with a client and you needed to know an answer to a question, enrolling on a course might not make sense. But a quick nugget of knowledge that you can easily access in your company wiki might be. What you are drawn to is determined by the context of your need.

Here are examples of questions that identify the pull forces:

- What does success look like when you solve this problem?
- How does solving this problem help your team and the business?
- Has anything helped you make progress towards solving this problem?
- Was there anything you tried that didn't help?
- What do you think would help you solve this problem and why?

Push and pull forces work together to motivate the employee to learn. Feeling incompetent at using a new project management tool rolled out across the company might be a push force, but there would be no pull unless you were persuaded that knowing how to use the tool will help you achieve your goals. If your learning doesn't help the employee progress towards their desired outcome, the number of courses you offer doesn't matter.

3. ANXIETY

The anxiety of what could happen (or the uncertainty of change) opposes the push and pull forces. This could be:

- **At the point of learning:** You're not sure whether learning better communication skills will make you better at your job. This could be because the value of the learning experience and how it will help you reach your desired outcome hasn't been communicated clearly. Alternatively, you might not be confident about your ability to learn something new. For example, 'I'm not good at networking. It's just the way I am.'

- **At the point of application:** The fear of applying what you've learned and getting it wrong is enough to put many people off learning in the first place, especially if you don't have a supportive manager or a work culture that embraces experimentation.

Here are examples of questions that identify the factors inducing anxiety:

- What concerns you about learning a new way of doing things?
- What's the hardest thing about trying something new to solve the problem?
- What questions run through your mind when you think about learning a better way of doing things?

4. HABITS

People can also experience inertia. This tendency to do nothing about an unhappy situation comes from an unwillingness to change habits. This could be:

- **Habits of learning:** How do they currently learn? How do they go about finding answers to these questions? For example, when they encounter a particular problem at work, their habit might be to search first for the answer, but if your company only offers a two-day course rather than on-demand learning resources, the employee is unlikely to engage.

- **Existing behaviours:** Habits are hard to break, from how you manage your time to how you manage people. Without practice and feedback to support learning, people often revert to their old way of doing things. Understanding existing habits will inform how much practice and feedback you build into your learning experiences to drive sustainable behaviour change.

Here are examples of questions to uncover the habits at play:

- Can you walk me through how you currently do things?
- What do you do when you need to find something?
- How much time do you spend trying to find a way to solve this problem?
- What do you think holds you back from actively finding or trying a new solution that might resolve the problem?

Progress-hindering forces such as anxiety and habit are just as important as push and pull forces. These forces can be why your learning experience fails to engage employees or drive impact, just as much as getting the problem trigger or desired outcome wrong. For example, you might be unhappy with the structure of the one-to-ones you do with your team; however, the anxiety of trying a new way that might be worse or the effort required to change a habit you've had for years might hold you back.

Get out of the building (or away from your desk)

You've found your people to talk to, mapped out what you need to learn, prepared some guideline questions and scheduled the interview. Now it's time to get out of your metaphorical office cubicle and talk to your colleagues. *But what if I don't get useful answers? What if the conversation dries up and we're left awkwardly staring into each other's eyes? What if I'm doing it online and the internet cuts off? What if it's a complete waste of time?*

It's normal to feel a bit nervous before your first customer interview with a colleague you don't know. That's just the anxiety we discussed above, holding you back from applying what you've learned. The pull of finding the right problem to solve and practise over time will get you through that. Here are some tools and techniques to help you have enjoyable and insightful conversations.

Before the interview

Get your questions ready before the interview. Avoid leading questions and cut out questions that would result in a 'yes' or 'no'. Use open-ended questions to get your 'customer' to talk about the problem in their own words. The questions should act as an outline rather than a precise script. The questions should give you focus areas, but a great interview requires you to be attentive and curious throughout. Be prepared to riff on answers and dig deeper where necessary.

On the game day, make sure you've got your questions printed or accessible on your device. If it's in person, make sure you have an app on your phone or a device to record the interview (and make sure it's charged!). I've used the Just Press Record app on my phone to record and automatically transcribe the interviews. If you're doing it over a video call, you could use the built-in recording feature in Zoom or Google Meet tools, or use a tool like Otter.ai for recording and reliable transcriptions.

Set the scene

First and foremost, start the interview by thanking them for giving up their time. It sounds like common sense. Again, I wish it was. Reiterate the purpose of the interview. Check they're happy for the interview to be recorded. Assure them that what's discussed in the interview and the recording will only be shared with the rest of your L&D team; otherwise, it will be kept confidential.

Warm up

Start with soft-ball questions to build rapport. Get to know more about them and their role. Share more about you. Make them feel comfortable.

Problem discovery

Now dive into your questions. Go off script and follow up where you think it's necessary. Tell them to imagine that you're shooting a documentary, so you want all the details from the very first moment they experienced the problem to how it made them feel. No matter how small or silly something might seem to them, let them know it could be vital for you. If you're unclear with an answer, ask them to explain the point again.

The answers to these questions are where you'll find problems worth solving, so you should listen out for:

· What problem are they trying to solve?

· What's the when and where of the need? What's the context?

· What are the risks of not solving this problem for the individual, team and business?

· What motivates the employee, and what concerns them?

· How do they decide what they need to know to solve the problem?

· Anything that surprises you or seems emotionally charged.

Remember, the interview is an opportunity for you to learn about the problem, not pitch solutions. So keep the conversation focused on the problem they're trying to solve. If they start to suggest solutions, ask them why and gently bring them back to talking about the problem and underlying motivations.

You want presentation skills training? Why? *Oh, because you want to deliver better demos?* Why do you want to give better demos? *Oh, to convert more demos to won deals.* Why do you want to win more deals? *Oh, you're currently not hitting targets and want to be making more money.*

Wrap up

Thank your interviewee once again, and reiterate how much value this conversation will add to what you're doing. Give them a chance to ask you any questions they might have. If the interview went well and you think this person would be a great early tester of your solution, ask for permission to follow up. Ask them who else they think you should speak with to understand the scope and scale of the problem.

After the interview

Gather your insights and organize them based on the jobs to be done and the forces at play. Don't jump to a solution. Discuss the findings with your team:

- What was useful?
- What surprised you?
- What are the patterns?
- What contradicts your problem hypothesis?

Reflecting on these questions will help you interpret the comments into problems, and over multiple interviews, you'll start to see patterns.

Getting the most out of the customer discovery process involves combining insights from the interviews with supporting evidence from other sources. Let's say you've interviewed reps from an underperforming sales team; you might also look at sales activity data from the CRM, customer feedback surveys, or even comments on social media related to customer experiences. The supporting evidence helps you validate the problem and essentially build the business case for solving the problem.

Making customer discovery interviews a habit can help you make smarter people development decisions and solve business problems faster.

What next?

You've got a validated problem, and you understand the forces shaping the job to be done. Now we need to develop a plan to solve the problem.

In the next chapter, we'll cover how you can use a Learning Canvas to create, capture and communicate your plan to solve the problem in hours rather than weeks, all in a single page.

References

Blank, S (2020) *The Four Steps to the Epiphany: Successful strategies for products that win*, Wiley

Christensen, CM (2013) *Innovator's Dilemma: When new technologies cause great firms to fail (management of innovation and change)*, Harvard Business Review Press

Haider, A and Rasay, SJ (2021) Zoom's post-pandemic future draws mixed reactions from analysts, *S&P Global*, 3 June, https://www.spglobal.com/marketintelligence/en/news-insights/latest-news-headlines/zoom-s-post-pandemic-future-draws-mixed-reactions-from-analysts-64813779 (archived at https://perma.cc/5CAV-TNBR)

Ransom, D (2021) Michael Dubin makes his exit from Dollar Shave Club, *Inc.*, 15 January, https://www.inc.com/diana-ransom/dollar-shave-club-michael-dubin-omnichannel-direct-to-consumer-branding.html (archived at https://perma.cc/H3PG-JW2X)

04

Create an L&D strategy
with the Learning Canvas

A satisfied customer is the best business strategy of all.

MICHAEL LEBOEUF

Big problems are scary. Underperforming sales team. New disruptive competition. Changing market trends. All very scary. But what if you could break a big scary problem into smaller, less scary, solvable problems?

In the early days of SpaceX, Elon Musk faced a big problem when he was shopping for a rocket. Unsurprisingly, the cost of rockets was prohibitively high, even for a billionaire. They cost upwards of $60 million, and most people said that's unlikely to change. So what do you do? Have you ever bought an overpriced salad for lunch and wondered what's in it that makes it so expensive, and could you make it yourself for less? Well, that's exactly what Musk thought.

What's a rocket made of? It's aerospace-grade aluminium alloys, some titanium, copper, carbon fibre, and to avoid listing every part of a rocket, let's say a few other things. Then, just how you might buy the ingredients to make your own salad, Musk purchased these materials on the commodity market and built the rocket himself at almost one-tenth the cost of buying one. Problem solved. This is first princi-ples thinking in action (Foundation 20, 2012).

First principles thinking is when you break down a complicated problem into basic building blocks of what you think is true and then reassemble these blocks from the ground up to build a better solu-tion. It's how scientists approach problem solving. They start with questions like, what are we sure is true? What has been proven? They remove all existing assumptions, biases and known constraints to see the problem in a new light.

In this chapter, we'll talk about how you can apply the same approach to develop an L&D strategy that eliminates waste, maxi-mizes impact and solves your business challenge. Traditionally, this might take weeks, even months, to create. By the end of the chapter, you'll be able to use the Learning Canvas to capture the building blocks of your learning strategy on one page and create a plan in a matter of hours, not months.

What if Elon Musk was an L&D professional?

Many breakthrough innovations have resulted from boiling things down to first principles and then building up from there. For instance, Johannes Gutenberg combined the technology of a screw press – a device used for making wine – with movable type, paper and ink to create the printing press. At a time when many wrote off the manufacturing of cars as impractical and believed most people would continue to ride horses everywhere, Henry Ford asked, 'What would it cost to build this thing if I broke it down to its most basic materials and found a better way to put it together?' Ford invented the assembly line to reduce the time and cost to build his Model T and made travel easier for the masses.

First principles thinking is at the heart of many startup frame-works. At the beginning of a startup, the choices are almost infinite, resources are scarce, and uncertainties are plenty. By reasoning everything from first principles, startups can avoid the risks of assumptions and conventional thinking. Rather than sinking resources into opportunities that never materialize into something big, first principles thinking enables entrepreneurs to navigate the maze of decisions with some predictability by forcing them to focus on the most important questions.

How to apply first principles thinking to workplace learning

L&D is stifled by reasoning by analogy, somewhat the opposite of first principles thinking. As Musk explains, 'Through most of our life, we get through life by reasoning by analogy, which essentially means copying what other people do with slight variations' (Boog, 2013). When faced with complex problems, we default to thinking like everybody else and resort to the comfort of known solutions.

Let's take a look at an organization's decision to purchase a learning management system (LMS). If you've ever looked at job ads for a Head of L&D role, you'll often find one of the key responsibilities listed is the implementation of an LMS. Organizations start with the assumption that they need an LMS even before the L&D professional has had the chance to understand the problem they're trying to solve. How do you know an LMS will solve your problem? What is the business challenge you're trying to solve in the first place?

Further assumptions are thrown in the mix when the L&D team puts together a request for proposal (RFP) based on other LMS RFPs they've seen. What's worse, they make assumptions about the features they need rather than sharing the problems they're trying to solve. How do you know those features will solve the problem? What are those assumptions based on? What is the financial risk if it doesn't solve your problem? The corporate world is littered with unused LMSs.

This is just one example of the 'doing it because everyone's doing it' approach to L&D. There are unfortunately many more. Taking a first principles approach can free L&D teams from this conventional thinking. The customer discovery process we discussed in the last chapter helps you get to the first principles of the problem. Actively asking questions enables you to strip away assumptions and boil things down to their fundamental truths:

- What are the business challenges?
- Why do we need to solve these business challenges?
- When do we need to solve these business challenges?
- What is the cost of not solving these challenges?
- Who are the people who can solve these challenges?
- What are the right skills and knowledge for solving these challenges?
- How do we build the required skills?
- How do we acquire the required knowledge?
- How do we know once we have the knowledge and skills?
- What is the measure of success?

In these answers, you'll better understand the problem and the building blocks for your learning strategy. It requires some focused thinking to dig deep into the problem and discover those first principles, but it's worth every bit of time. If you dive into creating content or buying tools before discovering the first principles, you risk sinking time and resources into efforts that never drive real impact. The Learning Canvas helps you put first principles thinking into practice.

What is the Learning Canvas?

The Learning Canvas is a one-page template designed to help you deconstruct the elements of your learning strategy and then systematically optimize each one. It is a blueprint made up of nine building blocks that help you convert your organizational learning strategy into an actionable plan. The Learning Canvas is adapted from the Business Model Canvas first introduced by Alex Osterwalder and Ash Maurya's Lean Canvas (Maurya, 2012a, 2012b; Osterwalder and Pigneur, 2010).

The Business Model Canvas is like a blueprint for implementing strategy in a new or existing business. The Lean Canvas is more tactical for going from idea to successful startup with as little waste as possible. Both help you boil down what would have been a 50-page business plan that would have taken months into a single page that takes hours to complete.

In the early days of my startups, I would experiment with different business models using the Lean Canvas. Having experienced the first-hand benefits of a visual format that is concise, collaborative and easily shareable, I found myself adapting it to work with L&D and Leadership teams. The canvas allowed cross-functional teams to solve business challenges, quickly going from big picture to hyper-focus, confusion to clarity, and anxiety to agility. The feedback was overwhelmingly positive, and there the Learning Canvas was born.

How to create your Learning Canvas

The building blocks of the canvas capture the WHY, HOW, WHAT of your learning strategy on one page. Figure 4.1 shows the order I recommend for filling the canvas.

FIGURE 4.1 Learning Canvas

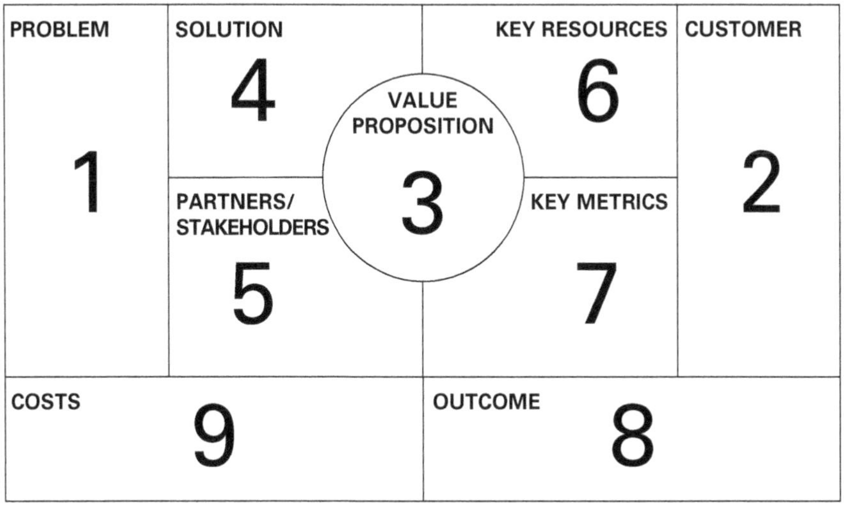

The WHY

The WHY is the motivation that aligns and drives the organization, individual and L&D team to invest time and resources in this learning strategy. This is made up of the problem you're trying to solve, who the problem affects, and the value they will get from solving it.

PROBLEM

After you've completed your customer discovery interviews, you will have a validated problem hypothesis. It's now time to define this problem in a statement that aligns everyone on the job to be done. The idea of framing problems using 'job stories' was accidentally developed by the team at customer relationship platform Intercom and later named by Alan Klement (2013), author of *When Coffee and Kale Compete* (2018).

Job stories build on the concept of 'user stories' commonly used in agile development. However, rather than framing the problem around user persona (e.g. as a salesperson), Intercom developed job stories so they could frame every problem around a job to be done, focusing on the triggering event or situation, the motivation and goal, and the intended outcome:

When _____, I want to _____, so I can _____.

Here's a simple example to demonstrate the concept:

When I go to the local supermarket to buy groceries ('Situation'), I want to find the cheapest available produce ('Motivation'), so I can save money on my shopping ('Desired Outcome').

In the same way, job stories can be used to frame the business problems you're trying to solve with your learning strategy:

When I have one-to-ones with my team members, I want to have better career development conversations, so that I can retain our best talent.

A well-written job story brings clarity and gets everyone on the same page. For example, you could add more contextual information to the 'when'. Compare the versions below:

1 When I don't know the answer to a product question...

2 When I don't know the answer to a product question whilst pitching a client on a video call and I can't ask my manager...

In Version 1, a workshop on product features might work, but for Version 2, it wouldn't. You would be better off with a tool that allows you to discreetly search and surface bitesize product FAQs within your video calling tool. You can also add information about the user persona to make the context richer. For example, instead of using 'I', you could use 'when client-facing teams...'. Enriching the situation with context helps you visualize the point of need better and develop more relevant solutions.

You can add a high-level job story and up to three smaller job stories that help resolve the high-level job story for bigger problems. For example, the high-level job story might be:

When I have qualified a sales opportunity, I want to know how to manage the rest of the sales process so I can win the deal and hit my quarterly sales target.

To solve this big problem, you might resolve the following smaller job stories:

When I am completing an RFP, I want to know all of the up-to-date product and company information, so that I can complete it to a high standard quickly.

When the prospective client negotiates on the contract terms, I want to understand the impact of those changes so I can reduce the back and forth in the negotiation process and reduce the sales cycle.

Once you've defined your problem hypothesis, you have your North Star. This is the business challenge your learning strategy aims to solve.

CUSTOMER SEGMENTS

With the problem framed, define the different groups of people you aim to solve this problem for. The combination of problem and customer forms the foundation of your Learning Canvas and drives all other building blocks. Your customers can be segmented by:

Job role   Segment your customers based on their position in the company (e.g. Account Executive, Customer Success Manager, etc) and their responsibilities towards specific business objectives. You can also segment based on the seniority of the job role, i.e. first-time managers, C-Suite.

Department   Target a team based on their job function, i.e. Sales, Marketing, Engineering, etc. For example, you're rolling out a new CRM, and all of the revenue teams need to be upskilled on it.

Location   Segmenting your customer by location will help you consider using cultural or business references of the targeted area and examples that will be personal and representative for employees who live in that area – for example, helping employees understand and adapt to new regulations in different countries.

Projects   You can segment cross-functional teams who temporarily come together for a project. The people involved in the project might require specific knowledge, instructions and nudges during the set timeframe to complete the project.

Skills   Go beyond business rules to segment customers based on skills requirements. The idea here is to connect the business challenge to a skills gap and then use relevant learning to close the gap for employees. For example, this segmentation can identify people who need to develop better communication skills or close skill gaps for low adoption of new technologies.

VALUE PROPOSITION

Your value proposition is essentially the 'what's in it for me?' for the customer and the business. It's the quantifiable benefit you promise, and they believe they will get if they engage with your learning strategy.

The value proposition can be captured in a short statement that helps visualize the finish line. If you solve the problem for your target customer, what will have improved for them and the business? In other words, what's the customer's job to be done and what's the benefit of getting it done?

The benefits could be:

- increased revenue
- reduced costs/waste
- increased process speed
- reduced errors/accidents
- reduced time to productivity

Here are a few examples of value proposition statements that capture the benefit for the individual and business:

> *For employees: Improve your sales conversion rate and win more deals.*
>
> *For business: Improve sales efficiency and hit revenue goals faster.*
>
> *For employees: Start working with clients within four weeks.*
>
> *For business: Get new customer support reps up to productivity within four weeks.*
>
> *For employees: Have better one-to-ones and engage your team.*
>
> *For business: Develop better managers and keep your best talent.*

The value proposition will help inform the marketing of your learning strategy to stakeholders and employees.

The HOW

The HOW is the actions you need to take to solve the problem and deliver value to your customers and the business. This is made up of what knowledge and skills are required to solve the problem, the partners and stakeholders that will need to be involved, and what key resources you'll use to deliver value to the customers.

FIGURE 4.2 FiveADay.com: Problem, customer segments and value proposition

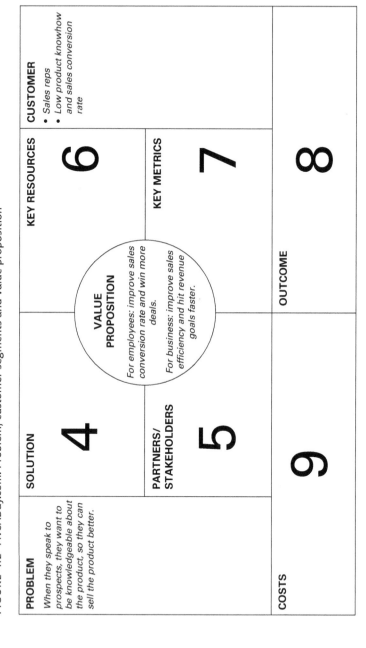

PROBLEM	SOLUTION		KEY RESOURCES	CUSTOMER
When they speak to prospects, they want to be knowledgeable about the product, so they can sell the product better.	4		6	• Sales reps • Low product knowhow and sales conversion rate
	VALUE PROPOSITION *For employees: improve sales conversion rate and win more deals.* *For business: improve sales efficiency and hit revenue goals faster.*			
	PARTNERS/ STAKEHOLDERS	KEY METRICS		
	5	7		
COSTS	9	OUTCOME	8	

SOLUTION

The value proposition describes the end benefit, while the solution describes how that benefit is achieved. It's important to point out that the solution isn't a list of courses or training programmes. It's the mindset, knowledge and skills the employee needs to solve the business problem. A learning strategy that doesn't help you gain the appropriate mindset, knowledge and skills is a waste of resources.

Mindset   Mindset is how you make sense of your world, your set of beliefs, and the way you think. It shapes your behaviours, how you respond to situations and make decisions. Mindset plays a critical role in how an organization tackles a business challenge and what it can achieve.

Knowledge   Knowledge is the facts, information and concepts you need the employee to know and apply to solve your business challenges. This can typically be acquired through reading, watching, listening, touching, etc. It can be shared from one person to another, and it can also be acquired through observation and study.

There are two distinct approaches to knowledge. Theoretical knowledge can help understand fundamental concepts and know-how about how something works, but practical knowledge gives you the techniques to actually do something. It's the difference between knowing how the mechanics of a car work and knowing that you need to turn the key in the ignition to start the car.

Skills   Skills are your ability to apply knowledge in a specific context to do something well. It's what your learners need to be able to do to solve the business challenge. Where knowledge is knowing that you need to pedal and balance to ride a bike, skill is knowing how to ride a bike.

Skills can be mastered with practice. For example, a Sales Development Rep can develop the skill of cold-calling by practising calling and speaking with prospective customers. Prior knowledge of a task can accelerate the time to build a skill. Reading Dale Carnegie's *How to Win Friends and Influence People* might give you an understanding of what is required to make people like and listen to you, but you can't develop the skill until you speak with people.

PARTNERS AND STAKEHOLDERS

Every learning strategy requires key partners and stakeholders to help you deliver the value proposition. Collaborating with the right partners and stakeholders is vital to ensuring employees connect learning to work and business performance. The problem you're trying to solve and who you're trying to solve for determines the partners and stakeholders you need.

Here are examples of partners and stakeholders you might need to collaborate with:

· Internal Subject Matter Experts (SME)
· External SMEs
· CEO
· People Manager
· IT
· Finance
· External Suppliers
· Team Leaders
· Contractors
· Business Partners

KEY RESOURCES

Key resources are how you will connect your learners with the mind-set, knowledge and skills they need to deliver your value proposition. What content and tools do you need? What would fit the customer segment and their context? Do the resources need to be created, bought, or do you already have them? These are just some of the questions to consider when filling this building block.

If you're thinking, 'isn't that just courses?', you're in for a surprise in the next chapter. We'll look at all the different resources you can find in your learning ecosystem to build learning experiences that help you deliver value.

FIGURE 4.3 FiveADay.com: Solution, partners and stakeholders, and key resources

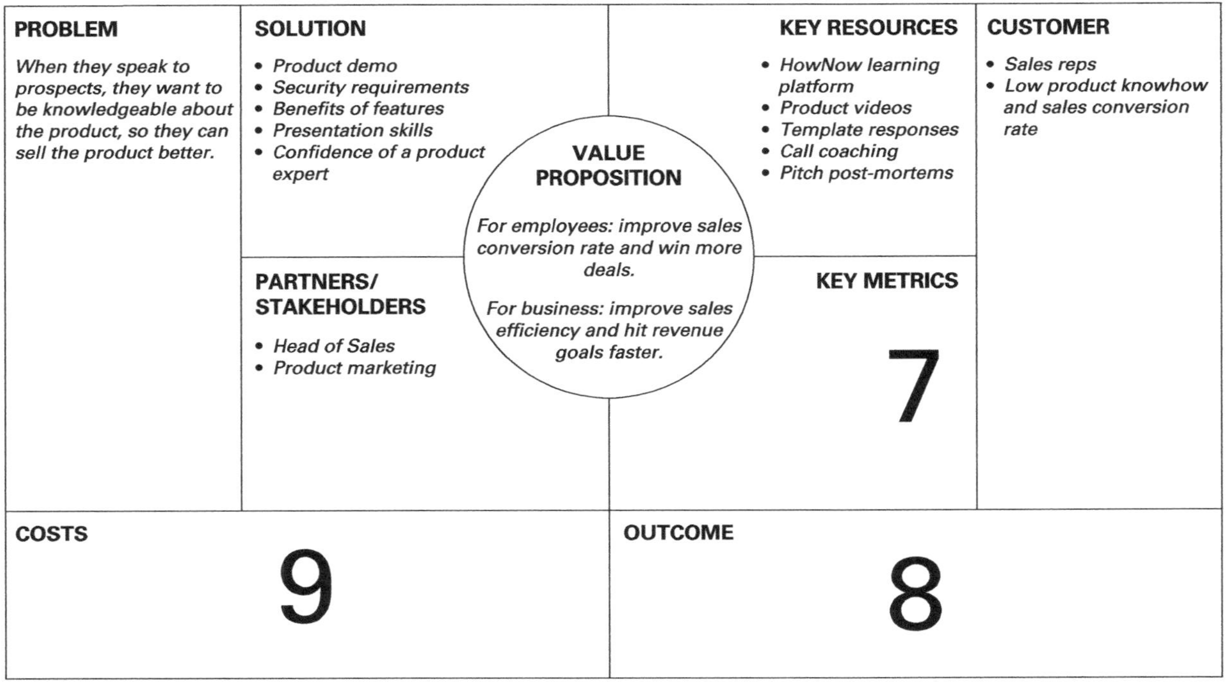

PROBLEM	SOLUTION		KEY RESOURCES	CUSTOMER
When they speak to prospects, they want to be knowledgeable about the product, so they can sell the product better.	• *Product demo* • *Security requirements* • *Benefits of features* • *Presentation skills* • *Confidence of a product expert*	**VALUE PROPOSITION** *For employees: improve sales conversion rate and win more deals.* *For business: improve sales efficiency and hit revenue goals faster.*	• *HowNow learning platform* • *Product videos* • *Template responses* • *Call coaching* • *Pitch post-mortems*	• *Sales reps* • *Low product knowhow and sales conversion rate*
	PARTNERS/ STAKEHOLDERS • *Head of Sales* • *Product marketing*		**KEY METRICS** 7	
COSTS 9			**OUTCOME** 8	

The WHAT

The WHAT is the results that tell you if your learning strategy has been successful. These building blocks are how you will measure the benefit of solving the business challenge you set out to solve, the key metrics that will inform you of your progress along the way, and the costs of solving the problem and ROI.

OUTCOME

The outcome is how you will measure the success of your learning strategy. For example, the outcome could be reducing your sales cycle from three to two months. Or to increase your customer Net Promoter Score (NPS) to 40. What is the outcome the business is willing to pay for? What is the desired outcome the employees are willing to invest their time for? Does the outcome drive business performance?

An outcome must be:

a measurable, and

b aligned between the business and the individual.

If the business challenge is to reduce the ramp-up time for new starters, solving it might reduce the time to productivity by 50 per cent. This outcome is both measurable and aligned between the individual and the business.

KEY METRICS

Outcome measures the end result and the success of your learning strategy. On the other hand, key metrics measure how well you're doing at delivering your solution. How many people have engaged with your key resources? How often are people using the learning resource?

Key metrics should be leading indicators that can show you in advance what the future might look like. Here are some examples:

· **Enrolments/Views:** How many people signed up? How many people spent time on the learning resource?

- **Shares:** How many people shared your learning resource? How many people shared what they learned from your learning experience?

- **NPS:** How effectively did the learners find it? Would they recommend it?

- **Mastery:** How did people perform on the knowledge checks? How successful were the practice sessions? How do the confidence levels before and after compare?

- **Time to improve:** How long did it take to see the improvement? Did it vary for different cohorts?

- **Stakeholder satisfaction:** Can the stakeholders see an improvement? Are they able to evidence it?

You don't need to track all of the above. Rather than overwhelming yourself with metrics, you should focus on one to three key numbers that tell you how things are going continuously.

COSTS

Cost captures the expenses related to delivering the value proposition and solving the problem. What's the day rate for the external expert? How much is it to develop or buy content? What's your budget for the learning platform? Focus on the most expensive parts and break down costs into fixed and variable. Combining the cost and outcome will give you the business case and potential ROI of the learning strategy.

What next?

Using the Learning Canvas, you will be able to create a plan to solve your business challenges. With multiple problems to solve, you'll first need to prioritize which plan to move forward with. But remember, each block in your Learning Canvas is still a hypothesis. You don't

FIGURE 4.4 FiveADay.com: Outcome, key metrics and costs

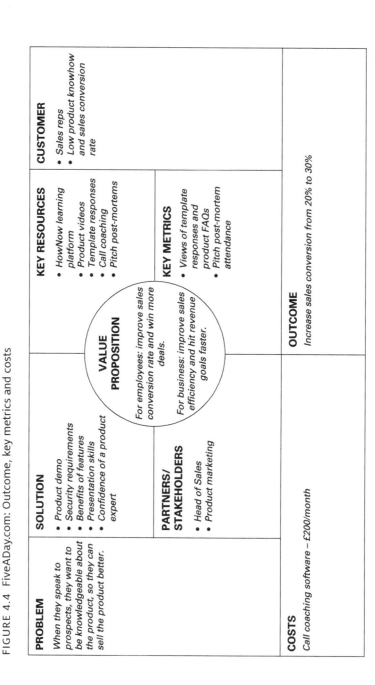

PROBLEM

When they speak to prospects, they want to be knowledgeable about the product, so they can sell the product better.

SOLUTION

- Product demo
- Security requirements
- Benefits of features
- Presentation skills
- Confidence of a product expert

PARTNERS/ STAKEHOLDERS

- Head of Sales
- Product marketing

VALUE PROPOSITION

For employees: improve sales conversion rate and win more deals.

For business: improve sales efficiency and hit revenue goals faster.

KEY RESOURCES

- HowNow learning platform
- Product videos
- Template responses
- Call coaching
- Pitch post-mortems

KEY METRICS

- Views of template responses and product FAQs
- Pitch post-mortem attendance

CUSTOMER

- Sales reps
- Low product knowhow and sales conversion rate

OUTCOME

Increase sales conversion from 20% to 30%

COSTS

Call coaching software – £200/month

know whether you have the right solution for the problem or whether the key resources will help drive the desired outcome.

Now we have a plan; we need to turn it into something tangible to start testing it. In the next part of the book, we'll look at the four steps to converting your strategy into learning experiences.

References

Boog, J (2013) Elon Musk: 'Pay attention to negative feedback, and solicit it, particularly from friends', *AdWeek*, https://www.adweek.com/performance-marketing/elon-musk-pay-attention-to-negative-feedback-and-solicit-it-particularly-from-friends (archived at https://perma.cc/VL7Y-6Y54)

Foundation 20 (2012) [video] Foundation 20, Google Ventures, Elon Musk, https://www.youtube.com/watch?v=L-s_3b5fRd8 (archived at https://perma.cc/ET5T-U43L)

Klement, A (2013) Replacing the user story with the job story, *JTBD*, https://jtbd.info/replacing-the-user-story-with-the-job-story-af7cdee10c27 (archived at https://perma.cc/CM3A-T7KS)

Klement, A (2018) *When Coffee and Kale Compete: Become great at making products people will buy*, CreateSpace Independent Publishing Platform

Maurya, A (2012a) *Running Lean: Iterate from Plan A to a plan that works*, O'Reilly Media

Maurya, A (2012b) Why Lean Canvas vs Business Model Canvas? *Leanstack*, https://blog.leanstack.com/why-lean-canvas-vs-business-model-canvas/ (archived at https://perma.cc/LFB3-XSJ7)

Osterwalder, A and Pigneur, Y (2010) *Business Model Generation: A handbook for visionaries, game changers, and challengers*, Wiley

05

Build a dynamic learning ecosystem

Don't find customers for your products,
find products for your customers.

SETH GODIN, MARKETING GURU

Over the past few years, neuroscientists, behavioural economists, and cognitive psychologists have achieved major breakthroughs in understanding how people learn, but this is yet to enter mainstream workplace learning. The research suggests that the timely delivery of just enough learning, personalized to the individual's need and incorporated into everyday work, is how people learn best. If you reflect on the last time you learned something that influenced your performance, this probably isn't surprising.

Lean Learning combines recent developments in educational pedagogy with Lean principles to create learning experiences that drive business impact whilst eliminating byproducts and processes that do not add value. Lean Learning helps you achieve this through a systematic approach that connects the right resource with the right person at the right time to drive the right impact.

That's a lot of rights. When you get them all aligned, you get learning experiences that maximize impact and minimize waste. It helps you develop a learning strategy as agile, fast and impactful as the organizations themselves. In this part of the book, we'll look at how to get each component right, starting with getting the right learning resources in this chapter.

From static library to dynamic ecosystem

Once upon a time, most of the world's recorded knowledge lived in the Library of Alexandria in Egypt. Today, knowledge is everywhere – on all our devices, in various formats, at our fingertips. Much like the world's knowledge, the knowledge your workforce needs also no longer lives in one content library. If it did, your employees wouldn't be tapping their colleagues' shoulders to ask questions or search online.

Training programmes and content catalogues are a big part of organizations' L&D offerings and budget spending, but they're such a small part of how employees learn. Whilst companies have been pushing training, employees have been pulling learning from elsewhere. That might be listening to podcasts and subscribing to a newsletter for one person, and joining a Slack community and dipping into just the relevant parts of an online course for another person.

People have the power to learn what they need and learn as they go. A Towards Maturity report found that 79 per cent of the online learning resources that people are using are not provided by their L&D function (Daly and Overton, 2017). People are not waiting for L&D to create a course for them to learn what they need. They're searching, reading, listening, watching and even creating learning resources when and how they want.

Learning at work will go on, with or without L&D, so you might ask, 'What's the need for L&D?' Don't worry, this is not when we chat about why you need to rethink your career. On the contrary, the need for L&D is more significant today than ever before. Every organization, team and individual exists within a learning ecosystem – a network of knowledge, skills, experts and tools inside and outside the organization. Although L&D no longer owns an employee's learning and development, they play a critical role in bringing together the learning ecosystem.

Take the conductor of an orchestra. They have one of the most visible roles globally, but most people don't know what they actually DO. Can't the musicians play without them? Yes, they can, but through their gestures, the conductors interpret the musical works with information such as how fast and loud to play. They keep the hundreds of musicians in time, aligned and together. L&D are the conductors of the learning ecosystem (with less arm waving and a lot less sweat).

Every organization has a learning ecosystem, just like every company has a culture, whether established deliberately or not. Learning ecosystems can vary in size and maturity. Do you remember studying ecosystems in biology at school? Ecosystems with higher biodiversity and interdependence tend to be more stable, with greater resistance and resilience in the face of disruption.

The same is true for the interconnectedness and diversity of your company's learning ecosystem. But unlike in nature, effective learning ecosystems are not organic. They result from an intentional effort that starts with deciding what to include in the ecosystem. Let's take a look at the different elements that make up a dynamic learning ecosystem.

Open learning resources

From business challenges to the tools you use every day – most of it isn't unique to your organization. Likely, there are already useful open learning resources available for it online, so it would be a waste of your time and resources to create new content for it. Open learning resources can be categorized in the following ways.

Industry insights

Learning resources on business, leadership, technology and much more from experts inside the world's best companies and reputable industry-specific publications, e.g. Increment by Stripe, Lattice's Resources for Humans, Drift Insider, Offbeat, L&D Disrupt by HowNow, JoshBersin.com.

How-tos

For most tools and systems we use at work, how-to resources are readily available. In many cases, they go beyond sharing guides and support about the product to provide useful resources about the overall domain, e.g. Microsoft Learn, HubSpot Academy, AWS Training.

Thought leadership

From podcasts and blogs to newsletter subscriptions, you can learn directly from leading thought leaders, e.g. Neil Patel on marketing, Lenny Rachitsky on product development, Reid Hoffman on scaling businesses, Ben Thompson on Technology.

Learning media/providers

Ebooks, videos, articles and workshops from reputable media brands such as TED, Bloomberg and FT, and skill-specific providers, e.g. Project Management Institute, CIPD, IDEO.

With knowledge being created faster than L&D can create content, including open learning resources in your learning ecosystem helps your people find the most recent and relevant resource at the speed of need.

Collaborative learning and knowledge sharing

There is much knowledge within organizations that is rarely captured or shared. As a result, when people leave the company, all of their knowledge goes with them. You have a leaky bucket. At the current rate of change, no organization can afford to relearn the things they once knew. No one person or group can bridge the chasm between the present level of knowledge and skills and the level required to seize opportunities. Organizational success in the 21st century will depend on our ability to learn collaboratively and share knowledge within and across organizations.

Collaboration is a powerful way of bringing learning into the workflow, where people have to pool together knowledge for a common purpose. They collaboratively learn more through active listening, thinking critically, reframing ideas, connecting dots and articulating their points. This approach helps you unearth 'who's good at what' whilst assisting employees in building strong relationships across the organization and fostering a strong sense of community, even if you're remote.

Here are examples of how you can put collaborative learning and knowledge sharing to work in your organization.

Peer-to-peer learning

At Google, 80 per cent of all tracked training is run through an employee-to-employee network called 'g2g' (Googler-to-Googler) (re:Work, 2022). The 6,000+ Google employees in this volunteer teaching network dedicate a portion of their time to helping their peers learn and grow through teaching courses and designing learning materials.

Peer learning can also involve learning from external partners and customers. For example, Toptal, the agile talent staffing firm, brought together 60 primarily tech managers and directors from a wide range of clients to explore their experiences working with freelance technical talent and how they see the opportunities, challenges and risks.

Wikis and knowledge bases

Often the knowledge your people need to do their job well is locked in the minds of others. Most companies realized this the hard way when the Covid-19 pandemic forced them into remote working. The unintentional osmosis-like learning that was happening in the office was gone. Some companies have used technology effectively to create company wikis and hubs that bring together their collective knowledge.

Fast-growing companies like GymShark and Depop use HowNow to quickly and easily capture tacit knowledge and make it available on demand everywhere they need it. Quite often, knowledge is transferred in communication tools like Slack. With HowNow's Slack Bot, employees can capture the knowledge directly from Slack and save it in HowNow before it gets lost in the flow of conversation. Next time someone needs it, they can search first rather than shoulder tapping or waiting around for answers.

Hackathons

Hackathons are an opportunity for employees to step outside their day jobs, collaborate with people across functions and learn from each other whilst working on a joint project. For example, at Microsoft's annual hackathon, an employee can have an idea with business or societal merit. Then others who share the interest apply to join the team to develop the business plan, create the prototype and present it back to the company. Winning teams are funded to build their projects.

Cohort-based courses (CBCs)

The name refers to an online course where a group of learners start simultaneously and progress through learning material together. CBCs are typically a mix of self-paced material, live classes with instructors, active community, breakout groups and collaborative project work. CBCs combine the social experience of being in a 'classroom' with the flexibility of online learning.

What makes them so special? MOOCs and self-paced courses are pre-recorded, one-directional, with no opportunities to ask questions and receive real-time feedback. In contrast, CBCs are bi-directional with instructor–learner and learner–learner interaction. CBCs focus on active learning over passive consumption. There is a sense of belonging and accountability to continue that comes from being a part of a cohort.

As a result, compared to MOOCs' notoriously low 3–6 per cent completion rate (Lederman, 2019), CBCs have seen an average completion rate of 85 per cent, with marketing expert Seth Godin and educator Wes Kao's four-week cohort-based course AltMBA achieving a 96 per cent completion rate.

The social interactions required for collaborative learning and knowledge sharing help people internalize what they learn. Through internalization, newly learned behaviours can become habits (Science Direct, nd).

Job aids and performance support

Job aids are the Robin to your Batman with a lot less spandex. They are tools, devices or instructions that provide just the right amount of knowledge and support to help you learn and perform a task. If you've ever followed instructions for assembling a bookshelf, you've used a job aid. Have you ever written down the Wi-Fi details on a sticky note for a colleague? You've created a job aid (Stringer, 2020).

An excellent job aid guides performance, minimizes interpretation, provides ready reference, and reduces, as much as possible, the need for memorization and recall (Carlisle and Coulter, 1990). They help summarize practical knowledge into smaller, accessible resources that can be used in the moment of need and adapted to new workflows.

So when's a good time to use a job aid?

- When the risks and rewards of the performance are high.
- When there is a time gap between formal learning and application.
- When a task is complex and contains several steps or many decision points.
- When procedures or tasks frequently change, and you don't want people to have to memorize things.
- When accuracy is critical, and the possibility of errors is high or risky.
- When tasks are performed infrequently so people may forget how to perform them.

With this kind of performance support, you can reduce the back and forth of questions within teams and enable employees to become more self-sufficient. It's a great way to reinforce what has been learned from more formal learning and even, in many cases, a solid replacement. Job aids are a quick and inexpensive way of addressing performance gaps and ensuring consistency of performance.

Job aids come in different shapes and sizes. Here are some examples of job aids and performance support.

Checklists

If the task at hand does not consist of steps that must be completed in a specific sequence, but consistency is critical, then a checklist is a good fit. A checklist can help a person perform 100 per cent correctly. For example, a 747 pilot goes over a checklist of every critical function before a successful takeoff. That's 100 per cent performance.

Templates

If a customer support rep doesn't know how to reply to a customer query, it doesn't mean you need to send them off on a three-day course. Template responses for frequently asked questions that are accessible on demand can help cut down customer resolution times. Templates are effective at streamlining your work for repeatable processes – sales presentations, FAQs, project updates.

Digital performance support

The average enterprise uses about 514 different cloud services across 10 different categories like sales, marketing, productivity, social etc (Brinker, 2017). As such, employees have the pressing need to learn on the go as they use these applications. Digital performance support systems can increase feature and software adoption through interactive and in-context guidance.

They provide just-in-time, on-screen support and guidance within the apps and tools you use every day – as if you have your very own digital nerd sitting next to you. They reduce context-switching and can help overcome performance hurdles faster. Digital adoption platforms (DAP) can be used to create interactive walkthroughs tailored to support first-time users and expert users while they accomplish their daily tasks in a system.

Flowcharts

Flowcharts can help make big business decisions and life's toughest choices. We won't go into the latter. They're an effective way to distil big questions or complex processes into neat yes/no answers. It becomes easier to communicate the process with someone unfamiliar with it, such as a new employee or an external team. Reducing the time needed to learn the processes enables teams to get the work done faster. Flow charts are also helpful for self-service troubleshooting because they systematically narrow the range of possible solutions based on a set of criteria.

QR codes

Justin Timberlake may have brought sexy back, but it was Covid-19 that brought the QR code back. QR codes can be used for more than ordering food from your table. They can be used to provide access to time-critical knowledge in the flow of work. Imagine you have to give someone CPR at work, but you're struggling to remember because the last time you did first aid training was 10 months ago, and you're also under a lot of stress. Rather than searching for what to do, you could scan a QR code on the first aid box, and it opens a how-to video. QR codes can do what digital performance support systems do for online applications but for the physical world.

Coaching and mentoring

Coaching and mentoring can have similar outcomes. Both incorporate practice and discussion as teaching methods, but the approaches are slightly different. You can bring in external experts for both, but a good manager needs to move along the coaching–mentor continuum. Let's look at how you can use coaching and mentoring effectively in your organization.

Coaching

In Dr Atul Gawande's TED talk (2017) on the importance of coaching, he recounts the origin of coaching in sports: 'In 1875, Harvard and Yale played one of the very first American-rules football games. Yale hired a head coach; Harvard did not. The results? Over the next three decades, Harvard won just four times. Harvard hired a coach.'

But you don't need to be an athlete or sports player to benefit from coaching. With a growing body of evidence, it's becoming increasingly clear that coaching can help everyone to improve. Workplace coaching can help people clarify goals, deal with potential stumbling blocks, and improve performance through one-to-one interactions over a defined period.

Coaching helps unlock the coachee's potential by predominantly asking probing open-ended questions to facilitate awareness and enable future self-directed learning rather than advising and telling. Given the rate of disruptive change, managers can't have all the answers, so coaching is a model in which managers give support and guidance rather than instructions.

As coaching is participative, people learn new habits more quickly as they're actively engaged and see positive results faster. When managers coach their team members or peers coach each other, it encourages collaboration and promotes teamwork. It can help nurture relationships with open and candid communication between them. It's probably no surprise that this leads to higher productivity and a more engaged workforce.

Workplace coaching can help be highly effective at driving professional growth and organizational progress (McGovern et al, 2001). At international law firm Allen & Overy, they found year-end appraisals and rankings had become a deterrent to the kinds of open and supportive conversations that employees needed to develop professionally and grow the company (Ibarra and Scoular, 2019). So they abandoned the performance review system and now upskill their leaders to engage year-round in coaching conversations with associates, providing real-time feedback on their work. Employees report that these conversations create a new and useful level of dialogue about their career development.

Mentoring

Like coaching, mentoring can help solve problems, foster collaboration and improve performance. However, it involves the mentor imparting their own knowledge, experience and advice to those with less experience in the same domain. Seventy-one per cent of Fortune 500 companies have mentoring programmes (Beheshti, 2019). A CNBC/SurveyMonkey Workplace Happiness Survey from 2019 found that nine in ten workers who have a career mentor are happy in their jobs, whilst more than four in ten workers who don't have a mentor say they've considered quitting their job in the past three months.

At the world's largest aerospace company, Boeing, they offer mentorship opportunities to potential leaders (Boeing, 2007). In the Boeing Leadership Center, these budding employees are partnered with senior leaders in the company to develop the skills they will need to take on the challenges of leadership. Similarly, at Fortune 100 company Caterpillar, they offer a more extended programme where younger employees are paired with senior leaders of the company for two to three years to develop specific skills they need to succeed in the field.

But mentorship doesn't need to be unidirectional based on organizational hierarchy. For example, General Electric (2017) has been promoting reverse mentoring for 20 years, with younger employees guiding senior executives with digital skills development. At BNY Mellon's Pershing (2018), they found that reverse mentoring was a great way to attract young talent to the company whilst helping the executive committee to be more transparent and seek input from people throughout the organization on many decisions (Jordan and Sorell, 2019).

Reverse mentoring has also been shown to promote diversity and inclusion (De Vita, 2019; Heidrick & Struggles, 2022). The global law firm Linklaters (2019) piloted a reverse-mentoring programme to improve leadership's understanding of minority issues, including those of LGBTQ and ethnic minorities. Cornell University's School of Industrial and Labor Relations found that mentoring programmes also dramatically improved promotion and retention rates for minorities and women – 15 per cent to 38 per cent compared to non-mentored employees (Beheshti, 2019).

Online courses

It's hard to enable learning at speed if it takes you months to create an online course for today's needs. With the booming creator economy, many tools can help produce high-quality content faster. You can shoot 4k resolution videos using your smartphone or use Loom to make presenter videos sharing your screen in minutes. Need a presentation? Pick a template on Canva and off you go. Or why not set up an account on Instagram for your company's learning brand and use the 'stories' format to create nano-courses.

Audio courses

Audio is having its moment with the rise of Alexa and Siri, the resurgence of podcasts, the popularity of voice notes and the recent success of Clubhouse and Twitter Spaces. Yet, it's an underused format in workplace learning. You can create audio courses faster and cheaper using nothing more than your laptop. They offer the learner more flexibility than watching video courses with options to listen whilst on a run or doing chores.

Personal learning budgets

MOOCs and microlearning courses help support self-paced learning. However, rather than purchasing the most extensive library of courses possible, look for the best of breed for each topic. Even better, allocate a personal learning budget to individuals and empower them to purchase the learning resources that would be relevant to their needs. Rather than buying a company-wide licence for a library of courses where most of it won't get used, why not just spend on the courses someone needs?

Allocating personal learning budgets might sound like an expensive affair, but on the contrary, you end up saving money as you only buy what you need. You can use a tool like HowNow to allocate budgets, manage requests and track spending, or do it all on spreadsheets to test it out. Either way, personal learning budgets are a great way to empower employees to own their learning and development, ensuring you get a better ROI.

Radically flipped classrooms

Most instructor-led trainings used to take place in a physical classroom. This was before Covid-19, and 'you're on mute' became a rite of passage. Once the global pandemic shut all classrooms, companies scrambled to adapt their training for virtual classrooms. Many L&D teams soon realized a two-day course didn't work as well online for the same period. Having to stare at a screen for so long and the pressure of staying attentive and maintaining eye contact was draining for instructors and learners. Studies have shown that Zoom fatigue was for real.

Given the popularity of the live instructor-led training format, you would be forgiven for thinking it's highly effective for learning. But actually, its popularity is because of its effectiveness in teaching, not learning. Both are not the same. There is a misconception that learning can be 'done' to someone, but in fact, it is something that 'happens' to someone. You can transmit knowledge but not 'learning'. Learning has to be experienced.

From an instructor's perspective, it's a convenient and efficient way to get their information out to many people. However, numerous studies have shown that it's a terrible way for people to acquire knowledge and actually learn. One of the significant findings from how humans learn is that actively engaged minds learn much better than students who passively listen to lectures.

Through a radically flipped classroom, we can actively engage learners. Minerva Project (2022), a Silicon Valley-backed startup building the future of higher education, calls this 'fully active learning'. Instead of using their live classes to disseminate knowledge, they do that before the class so the students can learn at their own pace, and then use the class time for learners to use what they learned with the support of peers and the teacher's guidance.

They'll use polls, quizzes, collaborative whiteboards, breakout groups and discussions to make the most of the synchronous experience in the live class. This is quite the contrast to an instructor speaking for hours with no interaction with learners, which might as well have been a recorded video that the learner could have watched in their own time.

So there you have it. There's more to your learning ecosystem than a few mandatory courses. Why does this matter? Because to the person with a hammer, everything looks like a nail. Now, replace 'hammer' with courses or training programmes. Different business challenges require different learning experiences. For example, the 2001 revised version of Bloom's Taxonomy (Armstrong, 2010), a framework categorizing learning objectives into varying levels of complexity, uses the following sections in this order from simplest to most complex: remember, understand, apply, analyse, evaluate, create (Anderson et al, 2001). In this framework, a job aid would be sufficient to help an individual remember something but a hackathon would be better for the highest level of creating.

The learning ecosystem provides L&D professionals with a framework to move beyond designing courses to designing more strategic learning experiences faster and cheaper. Your rate of learning will compound as people are learning from what they learn and building on what others learn, creating new knowledge together.

What next?

People don't need millions of learning resources. They need the right one. In the next chapter, we'll look at how you can connect employees with the right resources from the learning ecosystem at speed and scale.

References

Anderson, LW, Krathwohl, DR and Bloom, BS (2001) *A Taxonomy for Learning, Teaching, and Assessing: A revision of Bloom's Taxonomy of Educational Objectives,* Complete ed, Longman

Armstrong, P (2010) Bloom's Taxonomy. Vanderbilt University Center for Teaching, cft.vanderbilt.edu/guides-sub-pages/blooms-taxonomy/ (archived at https://perma.cc/C3EZ-BY2Y)

Beheshti, N (2019) Improve workplace culture with a strong mentoring program, *Forbes*, https://www.forbes.com/sites/nazbeheshti/2019/01/23/improve-work place-culture-with-a-strong-mentoring-program/?sh=7c8576dd76b5 (archived at https://perma.cc/YH2Z-THBE)

BNY Mellon/Pershing (2018) Reversing the generation equation: Mentoring in the new age of work, https://information.pershing.com/rs/651-GHF-471/images/ per-reversing-the-generation-equation.pdf (archived at https://perma.cc/5FBU-4LEB)

Boeing (2007) 1-to-1 learning, https://www.boeing.com/news/frontiers/archive/2007/ february/mainfeature.pdf (archived at https://perma.cc/6F85-D6XL)

Brinker, S (2017) The average enterprise uses 91 marketing cloud services, https:// chiefmartec.com/2017/06/average-enterprise-uses-91-marketing-cloud-services/ (archived at https://perma.cc/5HZH-NN22)

Carlisle, KE and Coulter, PD (1990) The performance technology of job aids, *JSTOR*, **30** (5), pp 26–31, https://www.jstor.org/stable/44425906 (archived at https://perma.cc/KN9P-8TZX)

CNBC (2019) Nine in 10 workers who have a career mentor say they are happy in their jobs, https://www.cnbc.com/2019/07/16/nine-in-10-workers-who-have-a-mentor-say-they-are-happy-in-their-jobs.html (archived at https://perma.cc/ TAA3-GT84)

Daly, J and Overton, L (2017) Driving the new learning organization, *Towards Maturity*, May, https://www.cipd.co.uk/Images/driving-the-new-learning-organization_2017-how-to-unlock-the-potential-of-Land-d_tcm18-21557.pdf (archived at https://perma.cc/Q3PN-G7HQ)

De Vita, E (2019) Reverse mentoring: what young women can teach the old guard, https://www.ft.com/content/53d12284-391f-11e9-b856-5404d3811663 (archived at https://perma.cc/UE65-83ZX)

Gawande, A (2017) Want to get great at something? Get a coach, *TED*, https:// www.ted.com/talks/atul_gawande_want_to_get_great_at_something_get_a_ coach#t-338186 (archived at https://perma.cc/9VVY-3H3E)

General Electric (2017) The benefits of mentoring: How to cultivate the millennial generation, https://www.ge.com/power/transform/article.transform.articles. 2017.apr.the-benefits-of-mentoring-how (archived at https://perma.cc/ 3Z5A-3C9G)

Heidrick & Struggles (2022) Press Releases: Study: Women and minorities value mentoring programs, but findings reveal opportunities for improved effectiveness, https://heidrick.mediaroom.com/2017-12-27-Study-Women-and-Minorities-Value-Mentoring-Programs-But-Findings-Reveal-Opportunities-for-Improved-Effectiveness (archived at https://perma.cc/3DHE-2BVF)

Ibarra, H and Scoular, A (2019) The leader as coach, *Harvard Business Review*, https://hbr.org/2019/11/the-leader-as-coach (archived at https://perma.cc/X6WE-BSQD)

Jordan, J and Sorell, M (2019) Why reverse mentoring works and how to do it right, *Harvard Business Review*, https://hbr.org/2019/10/why-reverse-mentoring-works-and-how-to-do-it-right (archived at https://perma.cc/VS3P-8TUN)

Lederman, D (2019) Why MOOCs didn't work, in 3 data points, *Inside Higher Ed*, insidehighered.com/digital-learning/article/2019/01/16/study-offers-data-show-moocs-didnt-achieve-their-goals (archived at https://perma.cc/EB3M-U4WH)

Linklaters (2019) Reverse mentoring – forwards, not back, https://www.linklaters.com/en/insights/blogs/employmentlinks/reverse-mentoring--forwards-not-back (archived at https://perma.cc/RP5W-9H95)

McGovern, J et al (2001) Maximizing the impact of executive coaching: Behavioral change, organizational outcomes, and return on investment, *The Manchester Review*, **6** (1), pp 1–31, https://www.performanceconsultants.com/document/maximizing-the-impact-of-executive-coaching.pdf (archived at https://perma.cc/UPN3-QV57)

Minerva Project (2022) Our approach: Fully active learning pedagogy, https://www.minervaproject.com/our-approach/pedagogy/ (archived at https://perma.cc/2ZUF-HDBV)

Mind Tools for Business (2018) Bridging the divide, https://mindtoolsbusiness.com/research-and-reports/bridging-the-divide (archived at https://perma.cc/WNC8-HGN4)

re:Work (2022) Guide: create an employee-to-employee learning program, https://rework.withgoogle.com/guides/learning-development-employee-to-employee/steps/introduction/ (archived at https://perma.cc/4KXB-VHA2)

Science Direct (nd) Social Constructivism, https://www.sciencedirect.com/topics/psychology/social-constructivism (archived at https://perma.cc/G6BT-PNFS)

Stringer, G (2020) What is a job aid? How do they create effective employees? https://gethownow.com/blog/what-is-a-job-aid-how-do-they-create-effective-employees/ (archived at https://perma.cc/G84N-V7PE)

06

Personalize learning at scale

When it comes to video and pretty much everything else, the more personalized the content, the higher the chances of conversion.

JOHN RAMPTON, FOUNDER OF CALENDAR

Most startups fail because they run out of money before finding enough customers that value their product and will pay for it. Similarly, most L&D teams fail because they can't find enough employees who find value in the learning resources they're offered, and so they don't pay for it with their attention. Finding the right customer for your product is a critical step towards success for start-ups and L&D teams.

The way companies connect with potential customers has changed over the last few decades. In 2004, 37-year-old Brian Halligan met a fellow student named Dharmesh Shah at the Massachusetts Institute of Technology (MIT). Amongst other things, they discussed the potential of technology to enable smaller companies to compete with bigger ones.

At the time, big companies would spend their marketing dollars on outbound channels – mass cold calling, billboards, TV and radio advertisements. This was significantly expensive for smaller companies, and they could rarely compete in a numbers game against the established, larger companies. However, Halligan and Shah (HubSpot 2017) believed that the growing amount of time people spent on the internet was quickly changing the game from one of numbers to one of engagement.

A year later, in 2005, they put their new ideas of engagement over advertising on paper and created a solution for businesses to reach and interact with customers. Neither knew it yet, but they had formed the basis of inbound marketing and sown the seeds of HubSpot (2017). Today, they're a multi-billion-dollar company with over 100,000 customers.

Inbound marketing in practice existed before HubSpot. However, they coined the term, wrote the playbook and lived by example. Outbound marketing focuses on pushing out messaging to potential customers, and inbound marketing prospects come to you for your content (i.e. blogs, whitepapers, social media and newsletters). If they engage, it might influence their purchasing decisions.

The outbound versus inbound battle has had more airtime than an Anthony Joshua fight – and we'll come to who wins later. But the way both strategies are used today in marketing is an indicator of how much has changed in the way we discover and consume things. These changes extend into the workplace, amongst many things affecting the way we expect to learn. L&D has a choice to make about using outbound 'push' channels and inbound 'pull' channels to connect the right learning resource to the right person.

Organization-driven 'push' learning

Traditionally, the organization drives most workplace learning. L&D assigns training programmes such as onboarding, compliance and leadership development to employees based on who is believed to need it. Typically the target audience is defined by simple business rules such as join date, department and job role, often resulting in learning experiences that are too generic to add meaningful value. This approach has given business-driven learning a bad reputation but with some lessons from marketing that can change.

Let's imagine we're trying to find customers for a high-protein cereal bar. We could advertise to everyone who already buys cereal bars. However, if we used additional data to target busy workers who go to the gym in the morning and don't have time to eat a healthy breakfast, we're more likely to find customers with a need that better matches our product. L&D can similarly leverage data from across the organization and outside to push learning to a more targeted audience.

The relevance of relevance

L&D can personalize organization-driven learning at scale based on data such as:

SKILLS DATA

Successful L&D teams use light-touch skills assessments and benchmarking to identify business-critical skills gaps. With this insight, they're then able to push learning that aligns individual upskilling with business goals. If our current proficiency level is low, the learning content might be too unfamiliar or complex, requiring lots of new things to be processed simultaneously and overloading our working memory.

PERFORMANCE DATA

Learning should drive performance. Why not segment your audience based on performance gaps? For example, if you're trying to improve the customer satisfaction score for your support reps, you could use data from the helpdesk software to only target reps who have a score lower than the benchmark. Or you could use data from your task management tool to segment people who repeatedly miss deadlines on tasks and support them with relevant learning.

CAREER DATA

Career data can provide insight into what a person has done and what they desire to do. Let's say your company uses Salesforce as its CRM. Rather than putting all new starters through Salesforce training, you can use their previous work history data to only target people who have not used the system before. You can also use employees' expression of interest in job roles in your talent management system or internal job board to push learning relevant to their desired career progression.

BEHAVIOURAL DATA

Previously you had to stand beside an employee to understand their actions; technology now enables us to digitally and objectively quantify behaviours. For example, to counter the risk of burnout, you might push relevant learning resources to people who are sending emails after office hours or people who schedule back-to-back meetings without a break. Another example is using sentiment analysis data from emails to segment people who use a negative tone.

EXTERNAL BENCHMARK DATA

Leverage benchmarking data to get insights into organizational performance in your industry and/or across sectors. For example, using job market data, you might find some skills are growing in demand for specific job roles in your industry. You can use data to segment a target audience consisting of the affected job roles.

Employee-driven 'pull' learning

When self-driven, learning is underpinned by both need and personal interest, resulting in better retention and recall of knowledge over time and a higher probability of application. It's comparable to how content marketing generates six times more purchases than traditional ads. People proactively researching a solution are more likely to take action than people interrupted by ads. With pull learning, people become infinite learners, continuously seeking out learning resources to meet their changing needs.

A report from McKinsey (2012) found that knowledge workers spend 20 per cent of their time looking for the knowledge they need to do their job. That's a day a week. What more could your people achieve with 48 more days a year? L&D can resolve this challenge by guiding employees to take better control of their learning. Relevance and autonomy are catalysts for the pull movement, and L&D can enable this by providing curation and on-demand access.

Curation is the new content creation

We're in the post-content age, and content overload has counterintuitively made it harder, not easier, to learn. Have you ever scrolled through Netflix looking for something to watch, and then the next thing you know, you've been doing it for 30 minutes, and you're too exhausted to watch anything? That's decision fatigue.

The burden of choice results in inaction. Employees are suffering the same. Every day they face the pressure of making decisions. When you throw a enormous library and an internet-load of content into the mix and ask them to find and decide what to learn, what do you think happens? Not much.

Once upon a time, Bill Gates wrote an essay titled 'Content is King' (1996). In today's content-rich world, curation is Queen, and it is her reign. Here's why:

- **Curation is faster and cheaper.** On average, developing one hour of eLearning content takes 197 hours and costs $30,000 (ATD, 2021). Curation can take a few minutes and cost you nothing.

- **Curation is agile and minimizes risk.** When you're creating a training programme, there's often the risk that it's no longer relevant by the time you launch. Or the programme that took you months doesn't drive the desired impact. In both scenarios, you waste a lot of resources. However, with curation, you respond to today's needs today, and if the learning resource doesn't help, you can find something else without losing much money or time.

- **Curation is reliable and scalable.** Curation ensures that the content has been reviewed and verified by a human who understands your problems. It's easier to upskill others in the organization on curation rather than content creation; therefore, it is easier to scale, even with a small L&D team.

Curation is critical for organizations to upskill people at speed and scale. But how do you effectively curate for learning?

STEP 1: AGGREGATE

Much like how making a mixtape for your high school sweetheart starts with you gathering all of the songs they like, curating for learning starts with bringing together your learning resources in one place.

You can do this manually by storing links on a digital note or intranet, subscribing to RSS feeds, buying courses, following Twitter lists, signing up to newsletters and setting up Google alerts for topics of interest. Alternatively, a modern learning platform like HowNow can automate this process for you.

A common misconception is that the more content you aggregate, the bigger impact you'll have. However, fewer resources aggregated in a single searchable place is of more value to a time-poor worker than having more resources scattered across many places.

STEP 2: FILTER

From the songs you've gathered, you now pick out those that mean something to your special someone to include in your mixtape. You know, the song that was playing on your first date in the shopping mall food court. The song that triggers warm and fuzzy feelings whenever you both hear it. This is filtering. It's the step in the curation process that separates the critical from the unnecessary.

Essentially, people want the best content for their needs. A 2018 Think with Google report found that searches with 'best' and '___for me' had grown by 80 per cent and 60 per cent respectively in the previous two years. 'Best', in this case, can be determined with the help of your Learning Canvas. Is the learning resource relevant to the business challenge? Is it applicable to your target audience? Will it help drive the desired impact?

Filtering helps people focus on learning what matters rather than wasting time on high volumes of irrelevant content. You can simply start handpicking and organizing relevant learning resources into an internal newsletter, a listicle on your intranet, or a playlist in your learning platform. L&D needs to take the lead here, not as curators but as the enablers of curation. Community-driven filtering based on content shared, liked and commented on by peers enables you to curate at scale.

STEP 3: ENRICH

Now it's time to take your mixtape to a whole new level by recording yourself whispering sweet nothings before each song. This enriches your compilation with context that your sweetheart wouldn't get from finding the same songs elsewhere. It gives the songs a new perspective that only you could offer because of what you know. The sum is now greater than its parts, and that is the outcome of curation done right.

With the final enrichment step, you organize and present only the best of the content and the context and value that only you can add. This is often the hardest step but the most influential. It will require you to collaborate with internal experts. Done right, this step in itself is a powerful way to learn. Rather than memorizing facts, by collaborating with others to curate meaningful content based on specific topics, skills and challenges, we can collectively enrich the organization's knowledge each time we learn something new.

There are many ways to enrich filtered content. For example, you can add annotations that contextualize the material for your organization. Why does this matter? How is it relevant to their business challenge? Where can they find out more? You organize content into playlists and structure learning paths to connect seemingly disparate content and form new perspectives.

You can further enrich the content with skills tags that help the workforce leverage content that will drive the desired change. L&D can also use this to identify the redundant content (and corresponding providers/sources) that don't meet skill requirements and potentially save a lot of money by getting rid of the ones you don't need.

Push or pull? That is not the question

In marketing, companies successfully use a mix of outbound and inbound strategies to achieve their goals. The same is true for push and pull learning. Push learning is not about assigning learning because you think people won't learn anything if left to their own devices. Competent employees want to perform well. The power of push learning is to help those employees prepare for a challenge they might not yet be aware of.

Even the most self-aware, self-directed learners sometimes need guidance with new directions to grow. Guidance is not only important for the individual learner, but also for the company and the alignment of individual learning with corporate strategies. So the question is not whether organization-driven learning is important, but rather when and how it is.

Push learning can be a great way of triggering the initial reflection that influences the consequent pull learning. It plants a seed that can blossom with self-directed learning supported by a good manager and a well-curated learning ecosystem. On the other hand, pull learning can provide the data to inform organization-driven learning. For example, you could use real-time search data of what knowledge and skills are in demand to push more structured learning to those looking for it.

What next?

Connecting the right learning resource to the right person is the first step in developing a learning experience that can have a measurable impact. However, if an employee gets the learning resource three months after they needed it, they would have performed poorly and may end up developing bad habits. On the other hand, if they get it three months before, they might not remember much of it when it comes to the moment they need it.

Performance is what we do in the moment. When we connect the right resource with the right person in that moment, we have the potential to shape their performance for the better. In the next chapter, we'll look at how you can design learning experiences to shape performance in the moments that matter.

References

ATD (2021) How long does it take to develop training? New question, new answers, https://www.td.org/insights/how-long-does-it-take-to-develop-training-new-question-new-answers (archived at https://perma.cc/77GW-X7ZT)

Gates, B (1996) *Content is King*, Essay.

HubSpot (2017) Inbound marketing vs. outbound marketing, https://blog.hubspot.com/blog/tabid/6307/bid/2989/inbound-marketing-vs-outbound-marketing.aspx (archived at https://perma.cc/AV2V-NR4Y)

McKinsey (2012) The social economy: Unlocking value and productivity through social technologies, https://www.mckinsey.com/industries/technology-media-and-telecommunications/our-insights/the-social-economy (archived at https://perma.cc/EMU7-32AE)

Think with Google (2018) It's all about 'Me': How people are taking search personally, https://www.thinkwithgoogle.com/intl/en-gb/marketing-strategies/search/personal-needs-search-trends/ (archived at https://perma.cc/HJ9Q-YVBE)

07

Shape performance
in the moments that matter

*I used to think the timing was everything. I have since learned that
now is the time for everything.*

STELLA MOWEN, FOUNDER OF THE FIRST HILL

Waiting weeks for that yoga mat you ordered online to arrive, standing in the rain to hail a black cab, or only having three food delivery
flyers you got through the letterbox to pick from are all so last decade.
We haven't got the time or the patience to wait hours, let alone days,
to get what we want. With services like Amazon, Uber and Deliveroo,
we hit a button and expect results. We want our yoga mat, and we
want it now.

This is the on-demand economy, and it's changing the way we eat,
shop, play, discover new things, and even find love. It's also changing
the way we learn. For example, one animal is responsible for most of
the power outages in the United States – do you know which one?
There's a good chance that if you're curious enough, you'll search
online to find the answer. Today, we expect to get and use knowledge
instantly (although you might only ever get to use that answer in a
pub quiz).

Workplace learning offers the unique possibility of the immediacy
of purpose and real-world context, unlike school and academic

education, where we learn many things not knowing why or when we'll ever use them in our lives. Remember Pythagoras' Theorem? Most of us have never had (and probably never will have) a need to use it in the real world. The immediacy exists in the moments that matter, and when you design learning experiences for those moments, you can connect learning to performance faster.

What is a moment that matters?

A moment that matters (MTM) is an intent-driven moment where the employee needs to know something to execute a task well. At the MTM, the employee is the most motivated to learn. In these moments, they are likely to engage with the learning resource as they're in the context of applying what they learn. Why is this important? Because engagement is the primary requirement for learning to happen.

Imagine someone's trying to put out a fire in their house, and at that moment, you hand them a costly watch. The chances are they would have been happier if you had given them a fire extinguisher. However, they probably wouldn't be as glad if you gave them a fire extinguisher rather than an expensive watch for their birthday. When you connect the right person with the right learning resource, you get maximum engagement at the moment that matters.

The 'aha' moment

It's similar to designing products; you ensure the users experience the 'aha' moment as soon as possible. This is the exact point when users understand the value of the product, and then they typically commit to said product. For example, the moment you set up your first WhatsApp group and received a message from your friends. Or the time you ordered an Uber and minutes later you're in a car being offered a complimentary bottle of water on your way home.

When you connect the right learning resource at the MTM, it becomes an aha moment, an emotional reaction to discovering something of value. The employee can imagine how the learning might be relevant to their need, apply it, receive immediate feedback, iterate and reinforce a habit of learning. When there's no aha moment, you end up with inert knowledge.

Your people 'know more' from training, but as they can't apply it to real-world problem-solving, the organization can't see a measurable performance improvement. Several studies have pointed to the failure of training to produce more than partial success; as low as 20 per cent transfer into the job context (Baldwin and Ford, 1988; Georgenson, 1982; Newstrom, 1986). Learning that doesn't drive performance is a waste of resources.

The types of moments that matter

Each MTM signals the purpose, e.g. what and why someone needs to learn, and the context, e.g. where, when and how they will learn. Moments that matter can be categorized into two types:

1 **Micro-moment that matters.** These MTMs happen in the workflow – during a sequence of tasks. There are dozens of these moments in a working day. It can be learning to complete a task on a new or existing tool, asking how to resolve a client query, or practising for an all-hand presentation. These are like your sentences.

2 **Macro-moment that matters.** These MTMs happen throughout work life. It can be onboarding when they join the company, leadership development when they're promoted as a manager for the first time, or reskilling for a new role. These are like the chapters of your story, each made up of sentences.

Six influencers of a moment that matters

Understanding the factors that shape the moment that matters can help you design learning experiences that influence an employee's capability to pay attention, retain and apply what they learn.

Environment

The physical environment is probably the most obvious context influencer. Learning experiences designed for outdoor environments might need to consider weather conditions, not just for how they're delivered, but it might also determine what the employee is trying to do. Indoor environments can range from working at home to working in a factory or a store. The ambient temperature, noise, and illuminance in this context can affect learning efficiency.

Noisy environments can be distracting. Dark environments might need audio cues instead of visuals. A recent study found learning efficiency peaked in a thermoneutral, fairly quiet, and moderately light environment in the problem-solving process, while a cool, fairly quiet and bright environment worked best for attention-oriented tasks (Xiong et al, 2018).

With more teams going remote or hybrid, the organization has less control over the physical environment, and learning resources need to be flexible. The ability to observe and hear colleagues in an open-plan office can provide an opportunity to learn. But how do you offer the same opportunity to those at home?

The physical environment can also act as a trigger for self-directed learning. For example, you might have a QR code sticker next to a machine in a factory that surfaces a how-to video on your mobile device. Alternatively, you might just have a simple poster with a checklist next to it. Employees might also expect to access knowledge in their environment at the moment that matters. What would happen if you needed to use the fire extinguisher, but there were no instructions next to it?

Here are questions to consider when designing for environmental context:

- Where will the employee be at the moment that matters?
- What are the factors in that environment that can affect the employee's ability to learn and apply?
- What are the triggers for learning in the environment?
- How can the learning experience feel seamless in the environment?

Technology

At the MTM, a person's access to technology can influence where, when and how they learn. When you introduce a new software across the company, it's almost impossible to upskill employees on every feature before using it. Moreover, they might not need to know how to use every single feature, and it wouldn't be practical to do this for every tool they use at work.

Using digital adoption platforms (DAP) and electronic performance support systems, you can instead connect employees with just enough knowledge for them to complete their task at hand. With in-app product tours and context-relevant suggestions from tools like Google's Explore and HowNow's Browser Extension, technology can help make learning almost invisible and embed it into everyday habits and workflows.

If you have a learning or knowledge system that is poorly organized and difficult to navigate, this is an unnecessary learning barrier that costs your business money. Learning experience platforms (LXP) can offer a unified search that makes it faster to find anything in your whole learning ecosystem. In-app smart suggestions can altogether remove the need for search at the point of need – after all, the best kind of search is no search.

Technology can enable employees to learn from each other even when they're not sharing the same physical space. During the Covid-19 pandemic, the usage of communication tools such as Zoom, Microsoft Teams and Slack grew exponentially amongst remote and hybrid teams. However, it should also be considered that the devices people have access to determine how they can learn. Do they have the bandwidth to watch videos? Can they join from a video call? Do they have access to headphones?

Here are questions to consider when designing for technological context:

- What devices do they have access to?
- What sort of interactions do these devices suit?
- Are there unique device capabilities that you can use to your advantage?
- Do IT policies allow for access to external learning resources?

- How proficient is the target audience with technology?
- Does the technology give them access at the point of need?

Time

People are 'busy' and understanding their time context when designing learning experiences can help employees fit learning at the moments that matter. If something big happens in your industry in the morning, you might want to share updated learning resources the same day. If someone is stuck on a support query, they need to access relevant knowledge then and there, not three months before or after. You might push different job aids depending on whether someone's working the day shift or night shift.

Time can determine how someone learns. If they have free slots in their calendar, they might join a synchronous learning session. However, if the need for knowledge is time-sensitive, i.e. they're on a call with a client and need to know the answer to a question, asynchronous learning would be better. Time data can also be used to understand how long it takes to see an uplift in skills proficiency and empower individuals and businesses to pace their learning effectively.

If the data suggests, on average, that people learn for 15 minutes, then it doesn't make sense to curate or create hour-long courses. Show estimated completion times and progress bars to help the employee make informed decisions at the moment that matters. It can also help understand how many opportunities to practise can be scheduled and the duration of each option. Is it the length of a job rotation, or will it be a 10-minute simulation?

Here are questions to consider when designing for time context:

- How much time do people spend learning?
- Do people calendarize time to learn, supported by managers?
- How often do people learn?
- How long should the learning resources be?
- How much time to schedule for practice?
- What else is happening at that time?

Activity

Creating a proposal. Resolving a client query. Conducting a performance review. Making a presentation. The engagement in the activity is both learning in motion and a trigger for further learning. Activity characteristics such as accountability, autonomy, and the amount of challenge or demands are important for facilitating learning. A lack of accountability has been identified as one of the most frequent barriers to managerial learning (Longenecker, 2010).

The activity data can help design learning experiences for near transfer. A sales rep on a video call to a potential client needs support handling an objection they've just received, so live coaching whilst the call is in progress will probably be better than a course on product demos.

For someone installing machines in a manufacturing firm, an AR headset might be a better way to provide real-time, step-by-step instructions. For desk-based workers who need to follow a specific process workflow inside an application, e.g. an invoicing tool or CRM, the moment the employee takes an incorrect step, an electronic performance support system can provide immediate feedback to get them back on track.

The cognitive intensity of the activity can also determine how much cognitive load the person can take on. For instance, if the activity is cognitively intensive, the knowledge needs to be communicated shortly and succinctly to accommodate the employee's attention being preoccupied with the task at hand, e.g. short video, fewer words on the screen, minimal interface.

Here are questions to consider when designing for activity context:

- How complex is the activity?
- Are these activities digital or in real life (IRL)?
- Is the activity collaborative?
- How much autonomy do they have over the task?
- Is the activity passive or active?

Organization

An organization's culture can determine whether the employee can learn at all at the moment that matters. If psychological safety does not exist for employees to try new things, take risks, fail and learn, they'll never step out of their comfort zone because of the fear of negative repercussions (Noe et al, 2010). When the organizational context supports learning, and people are allowed to practise what they learn, there is an increase in self-directed informal learning (Choi and Jacobs, 2011).

In a collaborative team culture, people are more willing to ask questions at the point of need and share what they know to benefit team performance. Lawson et al (2009) found that informal socialization mechanisms (e.g. social events, communal areas, knowledge-sharing tools) played an essential role in facilitating inter-organizational knowledge sharing. Employees with high-quality relationships with their managers engage in more voluntary learning behaviours (Walumbwa et al, 2009).

Here are questions to consider when designing for organizational context:

- How does the organization value learning and learning from mistakes?
- Do managers provide opportunities to practise and feed back?
- What relationship does the learner have with managers and supervisors?
- Does the organization support informal and formal learning?
- What degree of cooperation exists within and between teams?
- Do communities of practice or knowledge-sharing networks exist?

External

What and when you learn is influenced by specific market forces and trends, whatever industry you operate in. They include new technology, government policies, economic conditions, consumer demands and competitive pressures. The Covid-19 pandemic is an example of an external factor that influenced what, when and how people had to learn. When organizations were forced to work from home, people needed support with managing their team remotely immediately, not a generic leadership course in six months.

Often headlines about technological advancements are accompanied by pictures of robots, but it's a lot subtler in most cases. A change in Google's search algorithm can influence what and when your SEO consultant needs to know to optimize your company's content for ranking higher on search results. The arrival of new technology can also increase competitive pressure and drive when and how quickly you need your people to upskill.

Changes in legislative requirements, such as health and safety regulations or the introduction of GDPR, can shift the priority of what you need to learn because of the severe repercussions of neglect by the employer. Timely delivery of relevant learning in the moment that matters can save the organization from possible legal action and, in some cases, direct financial losses.

Here are questions to consider when designing for external context:

- What has changed in your industry?
- What are the technological advancements your people need to be aware of?
- What are the legislative changes?
- How have consumer demands changed in your industry?
- How is your organization performing against your competitors?

When you learn is as important as what you learn. Considering the six influencers of those moments when designing your learning experiences can be the difference between people learning and applying what they learn or not. Remember, people are most motivated to learn at the moment that matters. When you connect them with the right resource at that moment, you get measurable performance improvements.

What next?

We've now gone through the steps to connect the right learning resource to the right person at the right time. But how do you know that's driving the right impact? How can you be sure it's solving the business challenge? What can you use to measure your desired outcome? In the next chapter, we'll look at how your learning experiences can generate proof of impact.

Oh, and the answer is the squirrel.

References

Baldwin, T and Ford, JK (1988) Transfer of training: A review and directions for future research, *Personnel Psychology*, **41** (1), pp 63–105, https://www.researchgate.net/publication/209409925_Transfer_of_Training_A_Review_and_Directions_for_Future_Research (archived at https://perma.cc/HJ5Z-8LA2)

Choi, W and Jacobs, RL (2011) Influences of formal learning, personal learning orientation, and supportive learning environment on informal learning, *Human Resource Development Quarterly*, **22**, pp 239–57

Georgenson, DL (1982) The problem of transfer calls for partnership, *Training & Development Journal*, **36** (10), pp 75–78

Lawson et al (2009) Knowledge sharing in interorganizational product development teams: The effect of formal and informal socialization mechanisms, *Journal of Product Innovation Management*, **26** (2), pp 156–72

Longenecker, CO (2010) Coaching for better results: Key practices of high-performance leaders, *Industrial and Commercial Training*, **42**, pp 32–40

Newstrom, JW (1986) Leveraging management development through the management of transfer, *Journal of Management Development*, **5** (5), pp 33–45

Noe, RA, Tews, MJ and Dachner, A (2010) Learner engagement: A new perspective for our understanding of learner motivation and workplace learning, *Academy of Management Annals*, **4**, pp 279–315

Walumbwa, FO, Croprazano, R and Hartnell, CA (2009) Organizational justice, voluntary learning behavior, and job performance: A test of the mediating effects of identification and leader-member exchange, *Journal of Organizational Behaviour*, **30** (8), pp 1103–126

Xiong, L et al (2018) Condition-specific promoter activities in Saccharomyces cerevisiae, *Microbial Cell Factories*, **17** (1), p 58

08

Measure the proof of impact

Instincts are experiments. Data is proof.
ALISTAIR CROLL, AUTHOR OF *LEAN ANALYTICS*

Let's be real. Would you care how much time employees spent on a course if it influenced a measurable performance improvement? Would you care if they completed the course or not if it solved the business challenge? Probably not. Why? Because solving the business problem is what matters. In an organization where you track learning hours and completion rate, you end up valuing the person who knows an answer but not the person who actually applies what they learn to create a tangible outcome.

It's like if marketing teams were optimizing paid advertising campaigns for click-throughs, but no one was buying. So contrary to common L&D practice, learning experiences should be designed to continuously collect and analyse data that demonstrates impact, rather than just tracking learning activity data. If it has a measurable impact, scale it. If not, scrap it.

Almost every business function has been through a data revolution that has informed their practice. Marketing has transformed from Mad Men to targeted advertising. Operations are streamlining the process of building products and delivering them to customers. Customer Service can predict customers who might need support proactively.

However, according to the CIPD, 36 per cent of L&D teams evaluate their impact based on participant satisfaction, while 18 per cent evaluate their impact based on a change in knowledge or skills. Only 8 per cent assess the impact of their learning initiatives by assessing the wider impact on their organization.

With 70 per cent of L&D professionals reporting they felt pressure from the organization to measure the business impact of their learning (Baska, 2019), it's now L&D's time to use data to design learning experiences that drive measurable impact. But where do you start? What evidence do you need to collect? What data is actually useful? Let's look at the three types of impact data that will help you measure the impact of your learning experience.

Proof of knowledge

Proof of knowledge demonstrates what the learner knows as a result of the learning experience. This is commonly achieved through:

- **Tests:** A simple knowledge check to see how much they've understood. This can be a multiple-choice quiz or short-answer test.
- **Discussions:** A structured, pre-planned discussion between the experts and the learners to assess how much knowledge they have acquired from the learning experience.
- **Q&A:** An informal dialogue between an expert and the learner to assess their understanding of what they learned.
- **Knowledge sharing:** Learners can create blogs, videos and presentations to share what they have learned.

It's important to note that proof of knowledge is not proof of impact. Just because someone has understood what they need to do, it doesn't mean they actually know how to do it. The common mistake many L&D professionals make is not designing learning experiences that go beyond proof of knowledge to measure real impact.

Proof of skill

Proof of skill is how you know you are on the right track. It demonstrates what the employee can actually do as a result of the learning experience. Connecting learning to doing helps you see whether there is a measurable performance improvement or not. Finding ways to demonstrate acquired skills is both motivating for employees and valuable for managers.

Proof of skill can be generated in several ways:

- **Simulations.** This involves getting employees to apply what they learn in an artificial environment that resembles the real work context. It can be as simple as a live role-play exercise, or you can use virtual simulations to create an immersive experience.

  For example, Audi gets its employees to demonstrate their skills in a virtual dealership online (Patrick, 2018). They encounter challenging scenarios, including demanding and hostile customers. Depending on how they deal with the scenarios, a barometer will change to show the mood of the virtual customer.

- **Stretch assignments.** This is a project or task assigned to an employee, which is beyond their current competency or experience level. By pushing them out of their comfort zone, employees are 'stretched' and forced to adapt to the situation by applying what they've learned.

  For example, at Yelp, employees are offered stretch roles where they are given responsibilities just beyond their current capabilities to learn and apply new skills.

- **Projects.** By connecting employees with relevant internal projects, they get an opportunity to apply skills that they don't usually get to practise in their day-to-day. With a well-framed problem, projects allow employees to use their skills in real-world situations and challenges.

  For example, Google allows employees to use 20 per cent of their time to work on their own projects (Clark, 2016). This gave birth to Gmail, Google Earth, and Gmail Labs. Before Google, 3M was offering employees 15 per cent of their time, which netted 3M's most famous products to date, including the office favourite, the Post-it Note (Goetz, 2011).

- **Observation.** You can evaluate an employee's skills based on observations over a period of time in their work environment. Observations should be formal (planned) and informal (spontaneous) based on the employee's work. This approach allows you to assess skills in the whole context, and it is one of the most cost-effective ways as it doesn't interrupt employees from work, and you can assess multiple people at once.

  However, employees might be intimidated by the awareness that they're being observed, which may detract from their performance. One way to overcome this would be to perform the observations over time so that the employee becomes used to observation and begins to behave naturally again.

- **360 feedback.** With this approach, peers who work with the individual can evaluate and give feedback on their performance. The broader cross-section of people involved, the better – for example, a close co-worker, a manager, a client, and a business partner. The goal of the 360 feedback is to provide a balanced view to an employee of how others view their work contribution and skills.

  Using a simple form builder or 360 feedback tool, a manager can send out a survey to collect anonymous feedback on the employee. This can be quantitative feedback (e.g. skills rating out of a five-level proficiency level), so it is deliberately light-touch and easy to collect over time to track progress. However, it's worth collecting short narrative feedback as this will provide employees with more insights and motivation to improve (Harrison et al, 2016).

- **Portfolio.** This is a collection of work the employee produces that requires them to apply their newly developed skills. For a sales rep, that might be a demo recording. For designers, that might be marketing collateral they've designed. For a software engineer, they might build micro apps using the new programming language they have learned.

Any sort of proof of skill assessment is only as good as its assessor. They can be from within or outside the organization, but they have to be an expert in that domain with sufficient proof of skill themselves to review and validate someone else's performance. The experts do not need to be more senior in the organizational hierarchy. A junior team member might have stronger digital skills proficiency than a more senior, experienced member of the team.

The process of validating someone's skill should be positioned as an opportunity to give and receive feedback. People should not feel like it has career implications as it would remove the psychological safety required for people to learn and practise without the fear of negative repercussions. It's best to get three to five experts to validate the proof of skill to ensure reliable and objective evaluation.

Proof of performance

Proof of knowledge and skill are leading indicators that the learning experience will impact individual performance. However, it is proof of performance that captures a measurable improvement in business performance. Proof of performance is generated when the skill is applied in an organizational context and solves the business challenge. It's like a lock and key that fits and opens the door to business success.

L&D should know what problem they are trying to solve and know what it will look like when it's been solved. Are you trying to grow the sales pipeline? Are you looking to reduce customer complaints? Or increase employee engagement? The success metrics should be agreed upon with the business managers and stakeholders at the planning stage when you're completing your Learning Canvas.

With the right data, you will know if your learning strategy has made an impact on driving the desired outcome. In many cases, the business impact is not just down to learning; it's about finding an aspect of the performance that connects back to the learning.

Quantitative measurement

L&D professionals need to collaborate with stakeholders and data owners across the organization to access the metrics that demonstrate the desired outcome. For example, if the problem is a low sales conversion, you would need to find the owners of the CRM and work with them to get access to the sales data. You'll need to do this before you start building your learning experience once you've agreed on the metric in your Learning Canvas.

Start by getting pre-learning baseline measures of the KPIs you're trying to improve. Then track these metrics throughout to see the impact of the learning experiences. It's essential to measure the KPIs over a suitable period depending on the scale of the business challenge, not just after employees have engaged with the learning experience. Compare each measurement with the baseline measure to find the difference.

Here are examples of metrics that you might measure that signal business performance:

- revenue growth
- profitability
- customer satisfaction score
- completed tasks
- cost reduction
- fewer errors
- net promoter score
- new clients
- sales cycle
- time to market

A strong correlation between the learning experience and improvement in KPIs is important; however, it doesn't necessarily mean causation. L&D can once again borrow from marketing here. It's often just as challenging to attribute winning a customer to a specific marketing channel. If someone read a company blog but only purchased the product three months later when they had clicked on an ad, which channel influenced the purchase decision?

One of the tactics employed by marketing is A/B testing, whereby they compare the results of two (or more) cohorts of users who have been exposed to different variations of an ad or a landing page. It's like having a control group in a science experiment. You would compare one group of employees who have been exposed to the learning experience with another group who haven't, to see if it made a difference.

Qualitative measurement

With the recent focus on Big Data and AI, perhaps the pendulum has swung too far in the way of quantitative measurements. However, qualitative measurements can complement the quantitative data. It helps build a narrative that connects learning to business performance, and the insights can contribute to demonstrating cause-and-effect.

Qualitative measurement focuses on understanding how people make meaning of and experience their environment or world (Patton, 2002). If you think of the numbers from the quantitative approach as the 'what', the qualitative data gives you the 'how'. You can design to collect evidence of the outcome and then work backwards to assess the contribution to that outcome.

Interviews, surveys and participatory workshops can be used for ongoing monitoring and evaluation during the implementation of your learning strategy to produce real-time data on outcomes. Design these to assess what changed and why and encourage participation from different stakeholders. They should not be designed to assess whether or not activities were carried out according to plan.

The Value Proposition, Partners and Stakeholders, Customer, and Outcome boxes in your Learning Canvas will help you decide what information to collect and from whom. The information you collect should include at least two things:

1 **Outcome:** What behaviours have changed? What are the performance improvements? What impact has this had on the business performance? What was the outcome? How did it change?

2 **Contribution:** How (if at all) did the learning experience contribute to this change in individual and business performance? What influenced the change?

You'll find evidence of potential outcomes from the quantitative data to which the learning experiences may have contributed. In your engagement with stakeholders, try to substantiate these findings and identify unintended outcomes.

At HowNow, we implemented a sales qualification methodology called MEDDPICC to improve how we approach each step of the sales process. We upskilled our sales team by disseminating self-paced learning resources, followed by a series of live group sessions and role-play practise sessions. Within the first quarter, we saw an increase in our sales pipeline and a reduction in our sales cycle. Through interviews with reps, we learned they felt empowered by the newly implemented methodology, and they said it contributed to their performance, validating the contribution of the learning experience.

Better evaluation with triangulation

Both quantitative and qualitative methods have their limitations. But the solution to overcoming these limitations is not to shrug your shoulders and not measure the impact on business performance at all. Instead, use a combination of the methods so the limitations of one method are mitigated by data from another method. This approach is called triangulation.

The term triangulation is borrowed from geometry, where knowing the precise location of two points allows you to determine the distance to another object. However, in this case, you don't necessarily need exactly two different methods – you just need to seek alternative ways of verifying the results.

For example, from looking at the data in your learning platform and CRM, you find a strong correlation between sales reps who engaged with your learning resources and those who generated the most sales. You then interview the reps and the sales manager to collect feedback on whether they thought the resources contributed to their performance. You can also survey the new customers about their experience to see if there is evidence of behaviours influenced by the learning.

Triangulation isn't always necessary. The decision to use the method should be based on the risk of waste if you progress or scale the learning experiences without doing it, rather than how long it will take you to triangulate the data. This approach can help you iterate or pivot your learning experiences before it's too late, and inform future learning experiences.

Continuous learning culture requires continuous measurement

Measuring and evaluating impact is not a one-time event that happens at the end of a training programme. Impactful learning experiences are underpinned by evidence from start to finish. Rather than a 'one and done' approach, Lean Learning incorporates continuous measurement to ensure you're on track to driving the desired outcome. Continuous measurement is the foundation of continuous learning.

The Covid-19 pandemic forced organizations to cut back on anything that doesn't drive impact, which increased the pressure on L&D to demonstrate impact. However, the problem with using business performance as the only indicator of learning success is that by the time you figure out it's not working, it's probably too late. It's just as important to generate proof of knowledge and skills to correct course before you waste too many resources, even if the goal is to drive the desired improvement in business performance.

What next?

A winning learning experience connects the right learning resource to the right person, at the right moment to drive the right impact. When the four rights align, you achieve your desired outcome. But how do you know what's right? Over the previous four chapters, we covered getting the four elements of a learning experience in place. In the final part of the book, you'll learn how to iteratively get the four elements right and achieve measurable L&D success.

References

Baska, M (2019) Majority of L&D professionals feel 'growing pressure' to measure impact, *People Management*, 14 February, https://www.peoplemanagement.co.uk/news/articles/majority-learning-development-professionals-feel-growing-pressure-measure-impact#gref (archived at https://perma.cc/RD3U-GMF7)

Clark, D (2016) Google's '20 per cent rule' shows exactly how much time you should spend learning new skills – and why it works, *CNBC*, 16 December, https://www.cnbc.com/2021/12/16/google-20-percent-rule-shows-exactly-how-much-time-you-should-spend-learning-new-skills.html (archived at https://perma.cc/6X76-HSZH)

Goetz, K (2011) How 3M gave everyone days off and created an innovation dynamo, *Fast Company*, 2 January, https://www.fastcompany.com/1663137/how-3m-gave-everyone-days-off-and-created-an-innovation-dynamo (archived at https://perma.cc/7AMK-LH47)

Harrison, CJ et al (2016) Factors influencing students' receptivity to formative feedback emerging from different assessment cultures, *Perspectives on Medical Education*, **5**, pp 276–84, https://doi.org/10.1007/s40037-016-0297-x (archived at https://perma.cc/7QJV-Y6S4)

Patrick, D (2018) Audi virtual training: New gamification learning concept in the digital car dealership, *Clubs1*, 18 June, https://clubs1.net/2018/06/18/audi-virtual-training-new-learning-concept/ (archived at https://perma.cc/E3MS-PUKG)

Patton, MQ (2002) Two decades of developments in qualitative inquiry: A personal, experiential perspective, *Qualitative Social Work*, **1** (3), pp 261–83, doi:10.1177/1473325002001003636

PART THREE

Go

09

Start testing with your Minimum Valuable Learning

Think big, start small, learn fast.
CHUNKA MUI, CO-FOUNDER OF FUTURE HISTORIES GROUP

Just over a decade ago, two product designers were sitting in their San Francisco apartment, dreaming of starting a business but barely able to afford rent. Until one day, they noticed a big design conference was coming to the town and wondered whether people would be willing to pay to stay at a stranger's house rather than paying inflated prices for hotel rooms just down the road.

The duo decided to test the assumption by knocking up a simple website with a few photos of their loft room. Not long after putting up their place for rent, they had three guests, each paying in cash for the privilege of a single airbed in a shared space, breakfast included. Brian Chesky and Joe Gebbia's minimum viable product (MVP), AirBed&Breakfast, kick-started the development of what is now a $30 billion-dollar giant, Airbnb (Aydin, 2019).

A minimum viable product is a product that has the smallest possible feature-set to capture the attention and satisfy the needs of your earliest users. It lets you test your idea – or 'product hypothesis' – and get feedback fast with minimal investment and very few resources. Thousands of incredibly successful companies have grown from modest MVP beginnings.

What if successful learning experiences could also start small? You could spend months developing an expensive training programme only to find that it doesn't solve the business challenge. Or no one needs it. But what if you could build something that lets you know in a matter of days or weeks if you have something that's driving results or if you need to pivot to something else?

This chapter will look at how the MVP approach can be adapted to develop Minimum Valuable Learning: the smallest learning experience you can deliver that would quickly make a big impact.

What is (and isn't) a Minimum Valuable Learning

Picture this. You've never baked in your life, but inspired by the *Great British Bake Off*, you decide you want to start baking cakes. It's unlikely that the first thing you would do is enrol yourself onto a week-long course to learn how to make a three-tier, multi-flavoured wedding cake with icing and decorations. That would be an expensive and time-consuming approach, especially if you get to the end of it and you still can't bake.

Alternatively, given that the desired outcome is baking a cake, you might start with a free 15-minute YouTube video on making a plain Victoria sponge cake. This is your Minimum Valuable Learning (MVL). It helps validate whether you're moving in the right direction towards your desired outcome quickly.

The MVL must take you from where you are to where you want to go. The MVL must deliver the value proposition you added to your Learning Canvas, not just a part of it. For example, it is not an MVL if you only learn to crack an egg or make batter because you do not get the value you need from the learning experience. The desired outcome is to bake a cake, not to be an expert in cracking eggs. Also important to note, an MVL isn't a minimal viable course. It refers to the minimum version of the four parts of a winning learning experience: right resource, right person, right time and right impact.

The MVL will help you gather feedback as quickly as possible to improve the learning experience until it achieves your desired outcome. You might find you're struggling to get the batter soft and smooth, so you ask a friend who bakes or book a virtual class where you can ask the expert specific questions. Or you might think the video is just enough for you to learn how to bake, and now you're ready to learn about icing and decorations.

The benefits of starting with an MVL

The purpose of an MVL is to provide immediate value while minimizing development costs and gathering feedback that can be applied to improve future iterations until you achieve your desired outcome. This agile approach has significant benefits over the all-or-nothing approach.

Minimize uncertainties and risk

The traditional approach to L&D has been driven by what Eric Ries, author of *The Lean Startup*, describes as 'large-batch thinking', which delays the opportunity to test the learning experience and gather feedback. If we develop a learning experience to achieve X, Y and Z before we test it, it will generally take us longer than if we focus on X first, then Y, and then Z.

By batching these requirements together, a company either develops an elaborate training programme or does nothing about a business challenge until they can justify the time and resources to develop a full programme. By this point, it is often too late, and the training programme is loaded with uncertainties, risks and uninformed decisions. MVL shrinks the 'batch size' to just enough learning to deliver value and gather feedback, with fewer uncertainties and a fraction of the risk of an extensive programme.

Increase speed of learning

You can't help your teams learn at speed if it takes you months to create learning experiences to solve today's business problems. The

MVL enables you to avoid scope creep and procrastination whilst delivering value to your employees faster. The quick release of your MVL means lower development costs and faster response time to business challenges.

Once you launch the MVL, you'll be able to use the feedback to iterate or pivot in the right direction quickly. All this speeds up the overall delivery of your learning strategy. You could also simultaneously develop and test multiple MVLs against different groups and allow teams to iterate based on feedback in less time than it would have taken to build and deploy a big training programme.

Win stakeholder buy-in

The key to getting buy-in from stakeholders and securing a budget is to build confidence in your learning strategy and its ability to solve the business challenge. MVL is an effective way of demonstrating the value and making a business case for broader deployment with minimal resources, which increases the chance of receiving stakeholder buy-in.

Stakeholders want to allocate resources to learning strategies that positively impact the business, and the MVL is a tangible way of evaluating its potential. Rather than investing in a vague hypothesis, the MVL provides data to make an informed decision. Stakeholders can realize benefits without having to wait months or even years to see a return on investment.

Focus on what matters

With the traditional 'large batch' approach, L&D often build training programmes that try to solve many problems for many people but instead end up being too much or too little to actually solve the problem for anyone. The MVL approach helps you focus on only the learning that matters.

MVL forces you to have better clarity about the problem you're trying to solve, who you're solving it for, how you will do so, and the impact of solving it. With the MVL your focus is to deliver value with minimal resources rather than creating the perfect course or training programme, so your efforts are better aligned with the business.

Go slow to go fast

Change is hard. Have you ever noticed the avalanche of negative comments whenever a popular social networking app changes its design? People tend to have an adverse knee-jerk reaction to over-whelming big changes. However, small changes take people on a journey and create opportunities for feedback. Starting with an MVL rather than a revolution to disrupt current behaviours helps you build momentum faster.

Starting with incremental change might sound counterintuitive for learning at speed. On the contrary, quick wins early in the change process build the confidence and appetite for change. It turns early learners into champions who can advocate for the change and creates success stories to motivate everyone else.

The pitfalls to avoid when building an MVL

Ready to build an MVL? Great, but before that, let us look at the most common mistakes L&D teams make when they try this approach for the first time.

Overbuilding

Perfection is the enemy of progress, and this could not be truer for an MVL. *The course has to look beautiful. The videos must have high production values.* This is the opposite of MVL. It just needs to be enough to move the needle. Find resources rather than creating. Film on your phone or webcam, rather than using big film crews. A one-hour session rather than the five-day programme. MVL has no room for bells and whistles.

Over-minimizing

Over-minimizing is when you take the 'minimum' in MVL too far. You've cut back so much that you're not adding any value and just wasting people's time. It will be harder to get people back to test your future iterations because they got no value from the learning experience. Remember, it's not enough to upskill someone on cracking an egg if they want to bake a cake. MVL must have just enough to add value and start showing signs of solving the business challenges without slowing down the development process.

Ignoring feedback

Everyone should fall in love, just not with their MVL. If you don't collect feedback, or even worse, you ignore the feedback you get, then it's the same as building a long and expensive training programme. It's like turning on the satnav but ignoring the instructions. You'll get nowhere. Without feedback, you lose out on the biggest benefit of the MVL approach, and you'll be wasting time and money in the process. Get feedback, double down on what works, and cut what doesn't.

How to design an MVL that hits the bullseye

The MVL allows you to test the assumptions driving your learning strategy. Does the learning strategy solve the business challenge? Does the learning experience deliver the value proposition? Are you targeting the right audience? The MVL turns these assumptions into a tangible learning experience that your customers can actually engage with so you can test them with minimal resources, gather feedback, and see what works and what doesn't.

But what do you include in your MVL? Before you can answer this question you need to first convert your learning strategy into learning experiences. To help do this, I developed the Learning Experience Bullseye (LXB) Framework.

FIGURE 9.1 Learning Experience Bullseye Framework

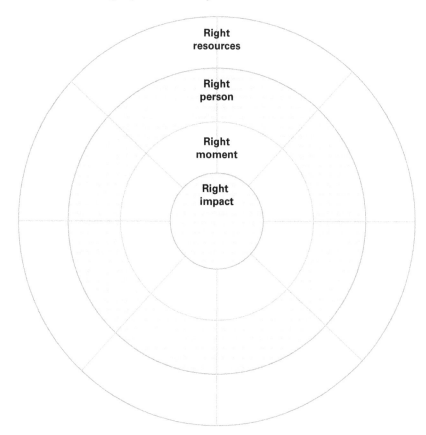

The framework is made of four concentric circles: outermost circle for right resource, the next circle for right person, then right moment, and the bullseye represents the right impact. The circles are divided into slices, each representing a learning experience. The bullseye metaphor is fitting because your learning experiences aim to get the desired impact – your bullseye.

Completing the LXB is a three-step process: Map, Score and Prioritize. Following these steps you can define your MVL and beyond.

Step 1: Map

The purpose of this step is to map your ideas for learning experiences onto the LXB. At this point, you're not thinking about the MVL.

You're exploring all the different learning experiences that could help you solve the business problem.

If you're doing this in person, you'll need some pens, sticky notes (preferably four different colours), and a whiteboard with the four concentric circles drawn on or a printout of the LXB template. Alternatively, you can do this virtually using a collaborative digital whiteboard.

You start from the inside out with the 'right impact' circle. Here you will define how to generate proof of knowledge, skill and performance to measure your progress towards the desired outcome. Will they need to do a role-play assessment? Will you measure the change in the NPS? How will you know the learning experience is helping you solve the business challenge?

FIGURE 9.2 Right impact

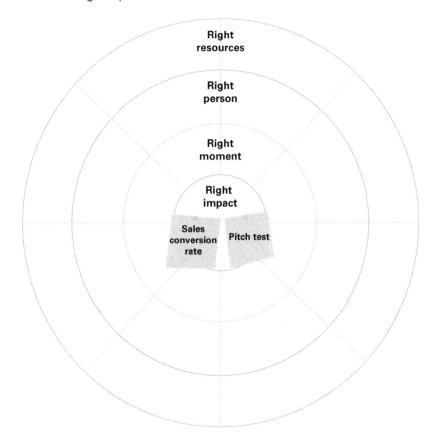

In the second-smallest circle, you define the moment that matters. What's the moment where, if you connect the employee with the right learning resource, you can shape their performance for the better? Think about the six influencers from Chapter 7: environment, technology, time, activity, organization and external. Is it when the person is on a call with a client? Or when they've just joined the organization? What are the factors that are influencing those moments that matter?

In the next circle, using the push and pull factors covered in Chapter 6, add how you'll get the resources to your right person at the moment that matters. Will they be able to access it on demand in their learning platform? Will you push it to them via email? The

FIGURE 9.3 Right moment

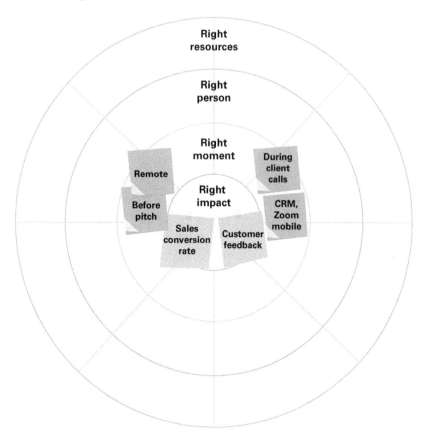

FIGURE 9.4 Right person

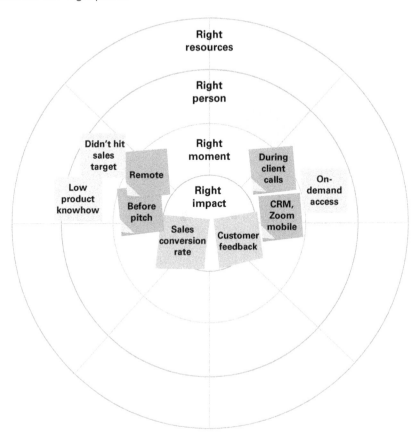

factors that influence the moment that matters will determine how to personalize the learning for the people who need it the most.

Then finally, you add the learning resources in the outermost circle. What content will help your target audience learn the skills they need? Think about your learning ecosystem and what you can use from there – mentoring from senior managers? Virtual Q&A sessions with external experts? Curated videos? Be specific about the learning resource. *What is it about? Where will you get it from? Is it paid or free?* Add a sticky note for each learning resource and align it to the push/pull options you added in the 'right person' circle.

With all your ideas for learning experiences mapped to the LXB, it's time to score and prioritize what to include in your MVL. When

FIGURE 9.5 Right resources

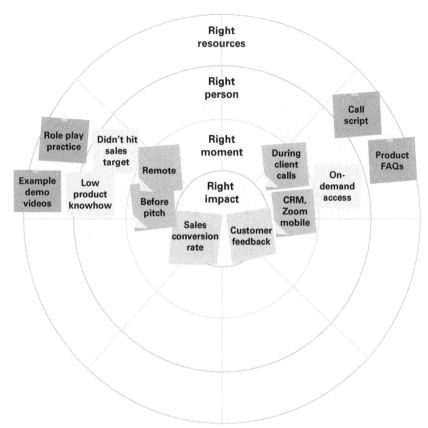

time and resources are limiting factors, effective prioritization is the difference between the success and failure of a learning strategy.

Step 2: Score

Each slice on the LXB represents a learning experience consisting of four aligned parts: resources, person, moment and impact. Although you don't have to fill all of the slices in the LXB, if you've been overflowing with ideas in the previous step, you've likely filled them all. To prioritize which one will be the MVL, we will give each slice an ICE score.

Coined and popularized by growth hacking guru Sean Ellis, ICE is an acronym for Impact, Confidence and Ease (Ellis and Brown, 2017).

It's a quick way to assign a numerical value to your ideas and prioritize them based on their relative value. Let's take a look at the three parameters:

- **Impact:** How much do you think this learning experience will help you achieve your desired outcome? Use a scale of 1–10 to give your score, with 1 being 'no impact' and 10 being 'very high impact'.

- **Confidence:** How confident are you the learning experience will drive desired performance improvement? Think about similar learning experiences you've delivered before. Use a scale of 1–10 to give your score, with 1 being 'no confidence' and 10 being 'very high confidence'.

- **Ease:** How hard is it to implement the learning experience? Think about every aspect of the learning experience: creating or curating, getting data to personalize, the complexity of the context, and how you'll generate proof of impact. Use a scale of 1–10 to give your score, with 1 being 'very hard' and 10 being 'very easy'.

Step 3: Prioritize

To calculate the ICE score, you then multiply the numbers. You'll end up with a number between 1 and 1,000:

$$ICE = Impact \times Confidence \times Ease$$

Once you have your ICE score, you add it to the outside of each slice in the LXB (see Figure 9.6). The higher the ICE score, the higher in priority the learning experience is. The learning experience with the highest score is the MVL you start testing.

ICE scoring should be a collaborative process that involves multiple team members, stakeholders and customers. It is an excellent opportunity to discuss and create alignment. In the end, it gives you actionable insights that can help drive your learning strategy forward. The prioritization should help weed out the high-risk,

FIGURE 9.6 ICE scoring

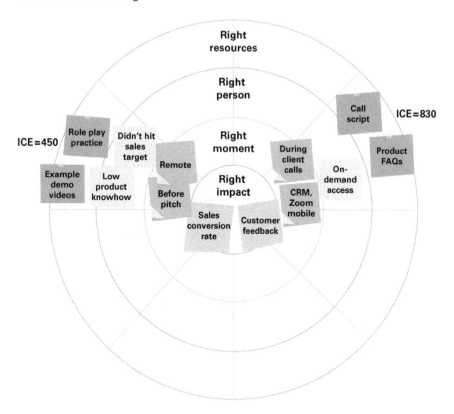

time-consuming and resource-intensive ideas and focus on ideas that can be tested quickly.

What next?

Now you know what your Minimum Valuable Learning should look like, it's time to build it. But unlike the traditional 'waterfall' approach, in Lean Learning, building the MVP is the first step in an iterative process to finding Learning-Challenge Fit. In the next chapter, you'll learn how to use the Learning Flywheel to test your MVL quickly and iterate until it works.

References

Aydin, R (2019) How 3 guys turned renting air mattresses in their apartment into a $31 billion company, Airbnb, *Business Insider*, 20 September, https://www.businessinsider.com/how-airbnb-was-founded-a-visual-history-2016-2?r=US&IR=T (archived at https://perma.cc/7SFU-VNJP)

Ellis, S, and Brown, M (2017) *Hacking Growth: How today's fastest-growing companies drive breakout success*, Currency

Ries, E (2011) *The Lean Startup: How constant innovation creates radically successful businesses*, Portfolio Penguin

10

Achieve Learning-Challenge Fit
or iterate trying

The only thing that matters is getting to product-market fit.
MARC ANDREESSEN, CO-FOUNDER OF NETSCAPE
AND ANDREESSEN HOROWITZ

It's 2012. Vancouver, Canada. History circled back on Stewart Butterfield. A few years earlier, he joined forces with some former team members and set out to build a web-based multiplayer game. Years passed. The game failed. But he broke out with another product he and his team had created by accident while making the game. The last time he'd done this, they had built Flickr, a photo-sharing service acquired by Yahoo (Geron, 2014). This time the product was called Slack.

Before they became one of the fastest-growing companies of all time, they started small. Butterfield and his team started asking around and calling in favours from friends at other companies to try the product. They listened to the feedback of the early adopters carefully, tweaking and refining the product as they went.

Each time the company received new feedback on Slack, they would address or implement changes based on that feedback and invite larger teams to try the product. Just seven months after starting, they announced their preview release. This was essentially their beta release, but they didn't want to call it that because then people would think that the service would be unreliable.

They invited teams in batches and watched what happened. Then they made some changes, watched what happened and made some more changes. They continued to wring every bit of feedback with a laser focus on learning from users and responding as quickly as possible. The app grew from 15,000 daily active users when launched in February 2014 to 1.1 million by June 2015 to 4 million in October 2016 (Novet, 2016). All of this without a multi-million-dollar marketing budget or a sales team. This is what product-market fit looks like.

Technology investor Marc Andreessen originally coined the term Product-Market Fit in his 2017 blog post 'The Only Thing That Matters'. According to Andreessen, product-market fit means being in a good market with a product that can satisfy the market. It's when your product serves your customer's unmet needs and delivers so much value that they're buying as fast as they can.

Product-market fit keeps startups focused on what matters: building a product that solves a real problem that a large enough market has. Without product-market fit, you risk wasting resources on scaling something that isn't working. L&D can apply a similar mental model to prevent the premature scaling of learning experiences before there is evidence that it is helping you solve the business challenge. When you achieve that, you've got Learning-Challenge Fit.

What is Learning-Challenge Fit?

When learning positively influences individual performance to help solve a business challenge, you have achieved Learning-Challenge Fit. Once you have defined your minimum valuable learning (MVL), it's time to start testing it for learning-challenge fit. Is it a learning experience that improves performance? Does it help solve your business challenge and drive the desired outcome?

For example, if your desired outcome is increasing the number of sales opportunities, is your MVL helping move the needle in that direction? Until you start testing, your learning experiences are not learning experiences. They're little more than a plan, some content and tools. You can change everything about your learning strategy until you achieve Learning-Challenge Fit: the solution, resources, target audience, timing.

All that matters is that you're getting closer to solving the business challenge. Until then, all the things about the learning strategy you captured in your Learning Canvas should be questioned because they're loaded with assumptions. Your MVL is the way to start testing those assumptions quicker without wasting resources. Once you achieve learning-challenge fit, you're ready to scale.

How to achieve Learning-Challenge Fit

Finding Learning-Challenge Fit is an iterative process that systematically improves how learning experiences are built and how employees learn. The two parts of the process have a symbiotic relationship, where both sides benefit from learning from the other.

The process can be captured with two integrated learning loops:

1 **Learning Experience (LX) Loop.** This is the process every employee goes through to learn the knowledge and skills they need to improve performance. It is made of four steps: learn, practice, feedback and share. This loop is derived from the last few decades of significant progress in the scientific understanding of how humans learn.

2 **Learning Experience Design (LXD) Loop:** This is the process the L&D team goes through to build the MVL. It is made up of three steps: ideate, build, test. This loop is based on the build-measure-learn loop at the core of the Lean Startup model (Blank, 2015).

Both of the learning loops feed into one another, building momentum with every turn like a flywheel. Every time an employee interacts with your MVL it generates information and data (qualitative and quantitative) that provides insights on how to improve the learning experience to create new value. This in turn drives the next iteration of the learning experience, which takes you closer to Learning-Challenge Fit.

FIGURE 10.1 Learning Flywheel

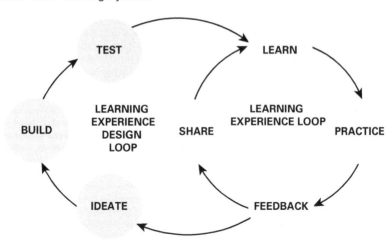

The flywheel metaphor reflects the difficulty of getting it off the ground, as the first test with your MVL has the most assumptions baked in. However, once you start testing and gathering feedback, with every turn, you'll convert uncertainties, assumptions and risks into learning that will improve your MVL and get you closer to your desired outcome. As a result, it takes less effort to keep the flywheel spinning with every turn.

The Learning Flywheel

We'll now go through the steps in the Learning Flywheel and see how each feeds into the next.

Build

In the last chapter, we looked at defining what to include in your MVL. In this step, your goal is to design and build your MVL based on the four components you defined in your Learning Experience Bullseye (right content, right person, right time and right impact). The purpose is to build the smallest learning experience that will move you closest to your desired outcome. If that doesn't work, you want to learn what worked and didn't work so your next iteration will be able to move you closer.

However, *build* doesn't necessarily mean build. It could be curating existing learning resources, setting up space for knowledge sharing, organizing coaching sessions, or developing job aids. The priority should be speed and value. If you're used to building long training programmes, you might be tempted to go big with your build because you can, but remember it is better to start small enough to add value to your target audience faster.

Test

What you build is an experiment with assumptions that need to be tested. In this step, you start running the experiment by making your MVL available to your target audience. When, where and how people will learn will be determined by your learning experience. For example, will you be pushing the content based on skills gaps? Or will employees be able to search from it on their mobile?

The 'Test' step feeds into the 'Learn' step at the start of the learning experience loop, so you must be set up to measure the metrics that matter throughout the learning experience. You'll also implement any necessary marketing to make employees aware of the MVL. It's important not to position your test as a 'test' to your target audience as people might think it's inadequate or not worth using yet.

Learn

This step marks the beginning of the learning process, whereby the employee engages with resources to acquire knowledge. For example, this could be from a YouTube video, webinar or mini-course. During this phase, you can track metrics such as open rates, attendance and completion rates to ensure employees are engaging with the resources, but bear in mind none of these metrics is enough to assume usefulness or performance improvement. If there is a lot of knowledge to be acquired, you should aim to generate proof of knowledge to measure the effectiveness of the learning experience.

Practice

You may have watched hundreds of hours of breakdancing videos, spoken to experts and discussed passionately on forums, but none of this means you can breakdance. You won't know if you can until you apply what you've learned and do it. Too often, workplace learning is focused on knowledge transmission, with very little thought to creating opportunities for practice.

Your learning experience should include at the very least risk-free opportunities for practice that are outside of the day-to-day work-flow. However, if the consequences of getting something wrong are minimal and irreversible, it is better to create opportunities for practice in the employee's real work context. For example, ask a sales rep to cold call a real prospect or get a customer success manager to run a product education webinar for new customers.

Feedback

The ability for an employee to gain feedback on their application of newly acquired knowledge as quickly as possible is as important as your ability to gain feedback on the effectiveness of the learning experience. In the practice step, you should generate a proof of skill and possibly a proof of performance that should provide two types of feedback:

FEEDBACK ON LEARNER

Most training programmes tend to include outcome-based feedback, which essentially tells you how you're doing. A basic example of this is a quiz that gives you a score. It's helpful in benchmarking people's knowledge level; however, it doesn't help the learner understand what they got wrong and what they need to do to get it right. As a result, feedback is used to mark the 'end' of learning rather than the learning experience itself.

The best kind of feedback helps employees understand where they are now and what they need to do to get where they want to be. You can achieve this by building opportunities into your learning experiences for corrective feedback that tells you how to fix what you got wrong.

For example, instead of just getting your score at the end of the quiz, you might also get feedback on what you got wrong and what you should learn to improve on that. Rather than being told in the practice session you performed poorly, you might receive peer feedback on what you could have done differently.

FEEDBACK ON THE LEARNING EXPERIENCE

The fastest way to get qualitative feedback on the learning experience is to speak to your learners. When did they use it? Did it help? How did it help? What was missing? Jump on a quick call with some of your learners to gather feedback. You might think this isn't scalable, but at this point, it doesn't need to be. You're testing your MVL, and once you know it works, you can figure out how to scale it. But until then, don't be afraid to prioritize speed over scale.

You'll also get quantitative feedback from the proof of skill and performance generated by your learning experience. Has your job aid on product knowledge reduced customer response time? Has the coaching helped improve delivery timelines? If not, then follow up with interviews with the learners and their manager and other stakeholders to understand the gaps in the learning experience.

Following the feedback step, the Learning Flywheel splits again with employees going on to 'share' in their learning process whilst the L&D team goes on to ideate what changes need to be made to the MVL, if any.

Share

Share is the next phase in the learning experience loop and plays an integral part in helping the flywheel build momentum. The obvious benefit of knowledge sharing is that it helps disseminate ideas, experience and knowledge to others in the organization to sustain and retain the knowledge in the business. With every turn of the flywheel, more learners will become experts who can contribute to building the learning experience, and people will feel empowered to learn as they see the benefits of others' learning.

The less obvious benefit of sharing knowledge is that it helps the employees learn even more as it forces them to recall and reflect on what they've learned. Sharing knowledge can spark debate and discussion, which provides a structure to make sense of learning so that concepts and theories become embedded in practice. Sharing with others and engaging with the community gives a feeling of importance, motivating further growth.

Ideate

Based on the learning experience feedback, it's time to decide whether you pivot or persevere. In *The Lean Startup*, Eric Ries describes a pivot as a 'structured course correction to test a new fundamental hypothesis' whilst persevering requires making smaller changes to your current hypothesis. It's a bit like poker. The amount of uncertainty reduces with every turn, and you need to decide when to raise, hold and fold.

Pivoting would mean changing the fundamental assumption captured in your Learning Canvas. Have you identified the right knowledge and skills to solve the business challenge? Are you targeting the right employees? Are you measuring the right outcome? However, iterating would require making changes to your learning experience by revisiting your Learning Experience Bullseye, and finding another a slice or two to test. You might update content in your job aid, turn it into a video or make it accessible on mobile too. You redefine your MVL and then go on to build.

With every turn of the Learning Flywheel, you'll gain momentum. The inherent feedback loops will help you optimize outcomes and reduce waste. The faster you go through the learning experience loop, the faster you learn what works and doesn't. The faster you go through the learning experience design loop, the faster you build the learning experiences to drive the desired outcome.

With this iterative approach to workplace learning, we embrace the notion that learning never ends – not for employees and not for

L&D teams. Instead, with every turn of the flywheel, we learn more. Every turn of the flywheel provides an excellent opportunity to get real-time data (both quantitative and qualitative) from actual employees and stakeholders about the effectiveness of the learning experience.

Each version of the MVL is an experiment. The faster you turn the flywheel, the faster you will learn what the employees need to learn to solve the business challenge. In the next section, we'll look at the catalysts you can use to turn the Learning Flywheel faster to accelerate your speed of learning.

How to turn the flywheel faster

At first, a flywheel barely moves. But when you keep pushing it, the effort eventually overcomes the inertia. Push by push, the wheel starts accelerating more until a point is reached where the momentum finally takes over. How fast your flywheel spins depends on how you manage force and friction. Force provides the positive energy that fuels forward movement and growth. Friction depletes energy and causes the flywheel to stagnate.

Not to scare you off with a little physics lesson, but organizations also have inertia to overcome before you can start turning the learning flywheel. Wonder if your company has inertia? When asked why you're doing things a certain way, if the response is some variation of 'we've always done it this way', and any alternative suggestions are faced with something like 'it's just the way it is' – that's inertia.

Overcoming inertia and accelerating your learning flywheel requires adding forces to areas with the biggest impact whilst eliminating friction points from your learning strategy. When you achieve this, you can deliver learning experiences quickly, receive feedback faster, and incorporate that into the next iteration – the shorter the iterations, the better the learning and communication within the team. Speed assures the fulfilment of the present needs and not what the business required yesterday.

Here are a few ways to apply strategic force and tackle unwanted friction.

The learning tech stack

Does your company have the necessary tools and technology to measure, support and continuously improve the learning experience? Technology can significantly reduce the time and resources required for L&D teams to turn the learning flywheel whilst providing the data and insights to get to the desired outcome faster. Of course, you can curate learning resources and create learning experiences that generate proof of knowledge and skills without the tech. Still, the right tech stack can exponentially improve your speed of execution and quality.

Without the necessary tech stack, it's impossible to personalize learning for 50 people in a meaningful way, let alone in an organization with 5,000 employees. Sharing knowledge around a whiteboard and learning from osmosis from those around us in a physical office may have been possible without technology, but in the new world of work where hybrid and remote teams are more of a norm, technology plays a critical role in collaborative learning.

Here are some of the types of platforms and tools you might include in your learning tech stack:

Learning management systems (LMS): Store courses, manage learning admin and track learning activity data.

Learning experience platforms (LXP): Bring together your learning ecosystem and support learning discovery.

Skills assessment tool: Deliver tests to measure skills proficiency levels.

Content authoring platforms: Create digital courses and learning pathways.

Virtual classrooms: Host live synchronous sessions.

Performance support systems: On-screen and in-app guides for driving digital adoption.

Mobile learning: On-the-go learning with micro-content.

Knowledge bases/wikis: Capture, share and browse company knowledge.

Community platforms: Facilitate discussions and collaborative learning.

Quiz builders: Create knowledge checks.

Digital credentials: Reward learning progress with digital certificates and badges.

Feedback/survey tools: Capture learner feedback.

Content libraries: A digital library of content assets like courses and eBooks.

L&D leaders must make sure that learning technologies fit into an overall system architecture that includes functionality to support the entire talent cycle, including recruitment, onboarding, performance management, L&D, real-time feedback tools, career management, succession planning, and rewards and recognition. You can buy these different tools and integrate them using APIs so they talk to each other, or you can use an all-in-one learning platform like HowNow to do it all in one place.

Alignment with business strategy

A clear, compelling and coordinated learning strategy will engage the organization, encourage collaboration and provide the energy to turn the flywheel faster. L&D needs to shape the learning strategy to support the implementation of the business strategy. For example, if the business goal is to launch a new product, then the learning strategy should be aligned to building the necessary people capabilities to make that possible. Sounds obvious? Well, only 40 per cent of companies say their learning strategy is aligned to business goals. For the other 60 per cent, there isn't a strong enough 'why' to turn the flywheel.

The clear communication of learning strategy is as important as its alignment to business strategy. The Learning Canvas can help with both. The single page format lets you frame the building blocks of your learning strategy around the business challenge that needs to be solved while sharing it with the wider business with little friction. When the learning strategy is relevant and accessible, it's easier to win over stakeholders and colleagues.

A co-ownership of the learning strategy between L&D and business functions can help build a better partnership that ensures alignment with business goals and reduces friction when embedding learning in the organizational culture. When the responsibility for ensuring learning happens, behaviour changes, and improved performance is shared among all parties involved, it becomes easier to learn about business problems, co-create learning experiences, and collect meaningful feedback data.

The power of psychological safety

Psychological safety was brought to the fore by Harvard Business School Novartis Professor Amy Edmondson when she researched teams in hospitals to find out what makes an effective team. You'd think that the better teams would make fewer mistakes, right? Wrong. Contrary to expectations, Edmondson found that high-performing teams reported more errors than low-performing ones. But it wasn't that they were making more errors; they were more willing to report and talk about them.

On the other hand, in the less effective teams, nurses remained silent about the errors they witnessed. Why? Because the team environment wasn't conducive to doing so. It wasn't psychologically safe. Edmondson's findings were echoed by a two-year study looking at more than 180 teams at Google that revealed five key dynamics common to high-performing teams. Number one on the list was psychological safety, which Google summarized as the confidence to take risks without feeling insecure or embarrassed.

Behaviour change often requires letting go of old thinking for new, and that can be scary. If people in the organization fear being ridiculed or making errors, they're less likely to share what they know, seek help, learn from mistakes, and receive feedback. People are more likely to develop and practise new skills and behaviours in a safe environment, where they don't have to worry about public failures that might affect their career paths.

Psychological safety is critical to tackling uncertainty that comes with rapid change, and left unaddressed will cause significant friction to turning the Learning Flywheel. You don't magically develop psychological safety; it needs to be deliberately cultivated like a bonsai tree. It can grow into something beautiful with care, but it can also be easily damaged with neglect.

Edmondson suggests three ways to build psychological safety in a team:

1 **Frame the work as a learning problem, not an execution problem.**
   When faced with a business challenge or working on a project, make it known that there is uncertainty and that you don't have all of the answers. Given the uncertainty, highlight the importance of having everyone's brains involved and voices heard. This framing helps nurture a learning mindset where the focus is learning what works rather than holding on to a pre-defined plan.

2 **Acknowledge your own fallibility.**
   It is not your job to have all the answers or micromanage all the work as a leader. You also don't need to put on an indestructible facade like a suit of armour, pretending that you don't make mistakes. Showing that you are human and make mistakes shows the rest of the team that they can be honest about what they don't know and what they can't do. Saying simple things like 'Correct me if I'm wrong' or 'I may miss something I need to hear from you' creates the safety for speaking up.

3 **Model curiosity and ask lots of questions.**
   Be curious about what other team members bring to the table. Be curious about what you don't know. As Amy Edmonson says, 'asking a lot of questions creates a necessity for voice' (Edmonson, 2018). And that voice needs to be heard when they're answering questions. Putting phones away in meetings and repeating what was said to show understanding, as well as non-verbal cues like eye contact and body posture, can encourage active listening. Hence, people feel valued and will contribute to the team.

Ironically, learning can also help develop the psychological safety required for more learning to happen faster. Feedback is a critical step in the learning process, and the more you give and receive feedback, the more people will feel safe to do it. Sharing knowledge also helps build relationships and foster trust, respect and openness, which creates psychologically safe environments.

Rewards and recognition

Changing behaviour can seem daunting, and it is human nature for the majority not to change until they really have to. For those who wish to change, the success stories are not there to inspire and learn from. This makes it hard to break organizational inertia and do something new, innovative and risky. Recognizing and rewarding success and publicly sharing these stories can help build the momentum of the Learning Flywheel.

REWARDS

Rewards are typically given by the leadership team and act as extrinsic motivation. It's important that rewards are given for successfully applying newly acquired knowledge and skills rather than for learning activities themselves. Here are examples of rewards:

- bonuses
- salary increases
- learning budget
- interesting projects
- mentorship opportunities
- gifts
- perks

Organizations typically shout about and share certificates awarded for learning completion, but not as much recognition is offered for people who have built in-demand skills and have contributed to solving business problems.

RECOGNITION

Recognition is about being meaningfully noticed by someone for what you've done, and it acts as intrinsic motivation. Recognition can happen at every level of the organization, from small teams to large divisions. It relies on every individual in the team rather than just team leads and managers. Recognition can motivate to do more of the behaviour that was recognized. For example, if an employee is recognized for learning the skills to solve a business problem of their own accord, they're more likely to do it again next time.

Here are some ways to incorporate recognition:

- give kudos on internal chat tools and external social networks;
- add time for recognition in weekly team meetings;
- shine a spotlight on success stories in the company blog;
- highlight how new skills contributed to business outcomes;
- encourage a culture of peer feedback and recognition;
- create a physical or virtual recognition wall with sticky notes congratulating exemplary colleagues.

Forcing functions

We experience forcing functions in everyday life. Ever tried turning on the microwave while it's open? You can't. That's a forcing function to protect you from being exposed to radiation. Barriers separating lanes on a motorway are another example of a forcing function to stop us from swerving into oncoming traffic. Forcing functions are an aspect of interaction designed to prevent the user from taking action without consciously considering information relevant to the action.

Most of the time, we don't fail to achieve our goals because of a lack of knowledge and how-to; we just haven't associated the right level of motivation to the outcome. Putting a forcing function in place creates motivation for taking action and ensures people have skin in the game, with consequences if they fail to show up and deliver.

Forcing functions can be used to build behaviour-shaping constraints into learning experiences, acting as barriers to distractions and creating demands upon the learner's attention so they can focus on what matters. We can avoid the scenario of frenzied clicking of eLearning courses to complete them for the sake of completion. Instead, force the application of learning that generates information and helps us improve Learning-Challenge Fit.

Making a training programme mandatory is a forcing function, but not always a good one. Why? Because although it forces you to complete the programme, it doesn't motivate applying what you've learned. Remember, learning should drive the behaviour change that improves performance, so the forcing function should be designed to drive behaviour change, not learning activity.

Here are examples of forcing functions to accelerate your Learning Flywheel:

- **Presentations.** If you know you have a scheduled presentation in two weeks during your onboarding, it forces you to reflect and apply what you've been learning. Presentations can be internal for the wider organization, or with potential or existing clients. For example, when onboarding a new sales rep, you might schedule their real customer call, focusing their attention on learning what they'll need for a successful first client call.

- **Projects.** Adding a time-boxed project deliverable as a part of your learning experience forces you to focus on things that you need to learn to create the deliverable in the given time.

- **Learning out loud.** Get people to share their progress with the wider organization or social networks. Writing a blog post, making YouTube videos or posting on LinkedIn can all be forms of learning out loud. This can help people learn faster as it forces them to reflect and get feedback. The by-product is you get to expand your network.

- **Company announcements.** People find motivation when they know there will be a real-life scenario to apply what they learn, and if they don't learn it, they will be left behind. For example, suppose a company announces they'll be moving to a cloud-based infrastructure in six months. In that case, this provides the L&D team and employees with the motivation to turn the Learning Flywheel faster.

- **Manager check-in.** A good manager can reinforce the importance of what people are learning and ensure it gets the attention required by simply checking in and recognizing progress. It's no surprise that employees are likely to consider something unimportant and irrelevant if their manager never asks them about it.

- **Learning pacts.** Two or more people can hold each other accountable for achieving the desired performance improvement. It forces ownership of goals and requires you to take responsibility for your actions. It's why people go to the gym or exercise with a partner. It might be too tempting to sleep in or skip your workout if it were only up to you.

- **Reporting.** Continuous measurement forces you to identify when you're going off track and course-correct sooner. Setting a regular cadence for business managers and L&D to discuss this and agree on actions forces you to collect data and do something with it.

With the types of lever discussed in this chapter, you can apply force to turn the Learning Flywheel faster whilst reducing any friction. However, don't try to use them all at once. Instead, get the flywheel moving and then experiment with different levers with each flywheel turn. Over time you'll find levers such as tech stack and psychological safety that will help you get the flywheel turning faster from the get-go and will have a sustained impact on the organization's learning culture.

What next?

The Learning Flywheel helps you iterate until you achieve Learning-Challenge Fit, but what good is that if it takes you so long that you miss the window of need? In the next chapter, we'll look at how you can use Lean Learning sprints to turn the flywheel in short time increments of two to four weeks and progress further, faster.

References

Blank, S (2015) Why Build, Measure, Learn – isn't just throwing things against the wall to see if they work – the Minimal Viable Product, https://steveblank.com/2015/05/06/build-measure-learn-throw-things-against-the-wall-and-see-if-they-work/ (archived at https://perma.cc/BT95-WHBC)

Edmonson, AC (2018) *The Fearless Organization: Creating psychological safety in the workplace for learning, innovation, and growth*, Wiley

Geron, T (2014) A look back at Yahoo's Flickr acquisition for lessons today, *TechCrunch*, 24 August, https://techcrunch.com/2014/08/23/flickrs-acquisition-9-years-later/?guccounter=1 (archived at https://perma.cc/BB6P-QN8J)

Novet, J (2016) Slack passes 4 million daily users and 1.25 million paying users, *VentureBeat*, 20 October, https://venturebeat.com/2016/10/20/slack-passes-4-million-daily-users-and-1-25-million-paying-users/ (archived at https://perma.cc/WD4P-725G)

Ries, E (2011) *The Lean Startup: How constant innovation creates radically successful businesses*, Portfolio Penguin

11

Deliver continuous learning with sprints

The important thing is not your process. The important thing is your process for improving your process.

HENRIK KNIBERG, AGILE & LEAN COACH

After the 2008 economic crisis, US-based NPR was hit by the cut in public radio funding. The development of new NPR shows had traditionally involved a lot of upfront time and money to create and prepare for launch. As a result, risks were high, and the ability to change based on feedback was slow. Yet, Eric Nuzum, the vice president of programming at NPR, was mandated to develop new programming with less. If Nuzum was going to make this work, he needed a new way (Johnson, 2012).

Whilst looking for inspiration, Nuzum found it inside their building, on the floor where Digital Media were sitting. For years, much like many technology teams, NPR's Digital Media team had successfully used the Scrum framework to deliver more value with fewer resources faster. Scrum is a type of Agile methodology. In other words, if Agile were the diet, Scrum would be a recipe. It gets its name from rugby, where a team tries to go the whole distance as a unit, passing the ball back and forth (Sutherland, 2014).

Nuzum and his team broke down their projects into a series of two-week sprint cycles, with a two-hour sprint planning meeting at the start. They would check in with each other every day with a standup meeting, coordinating who was working on what and identifying and removing blockers. At the end of each cycle, groups of stakeholders convened to review the work the team had completed. Once a project was done, the team members dispersed to begin new projects.

The switch to an agile approach resulted in developing some of their most successful programmess, such as the *TED Radio Hour*, *Ask Me Another*, and *How to Do Everything* – for a third of the usual cost. In the way the agile movement had swept through software development in the nineties and noughties as a backlash to top-down 'waterfall' product development, today we can find many such 'agile methodology' success stories outside the tech world.

In the previous chapter, we looked at the steps to learning-challenge fit. An essential aspect of that process is timing. You might have a 'perfect' learning strategy to solve a business problem, but if you can't execute it when it's needed the most, it might be too late. This chapter shows how we can use an agile-inspired Lean Learning sprint to implement our L&D strategy in a way that maximizes impact.

The Lean Learning sprint and what it's good for

At this point in the book, you have the steps to go from finding your business problem to achieving learning-challenge fit, but how do we implement this whilst minimizing time and waste? For that, we need a process that enables us to deliver value to customers faster whilst gathering feedback early and often so we can continuously improve what we do.

What are Lean Learning sprints?

Lean Learning sprints are time-boxed increments that enable cross-functional stakeholders to work together to go from ignorance of a business problem to a learning strategy that delivers value to the individual and organization. Like agile and design sprints, the Lean Learning sprints are an effective way to break down work into smaller chunks to deal with changing demands over time (Knapp, 2016).

However, what's different is that during the Lean Learning sprint, we'll go through the steps of the Learning Flywheel with the focus of achieving learning-challenge fit. In the way Scrum is a framework for putting agile methodology into practice, the Lean Learning sprint is a way to apply both lean and agile principles to the way you implement your L&D strategy.

Typically, the Lean Learning sprints are between two and four weeks long. The relatively short length of time might be a shock to the system if you are used to working on annual planning cycles and quarterly targets, but at the current pace of change, businesses can boom or go bust in that period, so you need to work in shorter increments. Most L&D teams find that two-week sprints often work best for them as it is short enough to get feedback quickly whilst long enough to complete work of meaningful value.

The benefits of Lean Learning sprints

Using Lean Learning sprints, we can release learning experiences quicker and receive feedback early to iterate on them and apply what we learn to future developments. Running a sprint is about building a shared understanding of the challenge across the relevant stakeholders. Once everyone knows what they're working towards, the sprint provides momentum, focus and confidence.

As cross-functional teams work together to make decisions and share daily status updates, it promotes transparency at individual and team levels. The fixed timeframe of the sprint prompts people to act faster, while follow-ups and decisions happen in hours and days rather than weeks and months. This flexibility allows us to course-correct and reprioritize what we're working on.

Assemble the right team for the sprint

So who should be in the room? Typically a sprint team should comprise five to seven people with diverse skillsets and from cross-functional teams. There are three main roles in the sprint team:

1 Sprint master

2 Challenge owner

3 LX team

Let's look at the responsibilities of each one and how they feed into the sprint.

Sprint master

The sprint master (SM) is responsible for assembling the team and keeping them on track. They lead the process and run the sprint meetings. When discussions go off on a tangent, the SM will bring it back to focus on the sprint goal or output. When you hit barriers that slow down the momentum of your Learning Flywheel, the SM will find the answers and help the team shuffle priorities to continue with progress.

The SM can be the L&D Manager; however, this is not necessary. The person who takes this role needs to be an influential leader and coach rather than a command-and-control master. When selecting your SM, it's more important that the person has the relevant skills.

For instance, SMs should be good at fostering relationships between people, so it helps if they are well-networked people in the organization. The SM also needs to actively listen to opinions and concerns, allow for discussions and debate, and manage different perspectives constructively. Find the person in your team who can do all of the above and give them the role.

Challenge owner

The challenge owner (CO) represents the 'voice of the customer'. They help the rest of the sprint team deeply understand the business challenge to be solved. The CO provides the North Star that the team is working towards. The desired outcome you're trying to collectively achieve. This role is the bridge between your target audience and the sprint team.

The CO needs to be the expert in the problem and provide insights that help shape the solution. However, they are not the authority in how the solution will manifest as learning experiences. The LX Team will determine this. The CO also helps make decisions regarding the priority of tasks in your backlog and provides access to data that generates the proof of impact.

The role can be filled by someone who will directly benefit from solving the problem. For example, suppose the problem was a low customer satisfaction score. In that case, someone from the Customer Success team could be your CO. Alternatively it could be an L&D business partner who works closely with the Customer Success team and deeply understands their challenge. The right person needs to be an expert in the problem.

When selecting the CO, consider their availability, as the role does need a significant time investment during the sprints, responding to questions, providing data where required, and attending the sprint meetings. It's important to set the expectations from the get-go to avoid it from becoming a blocker, especially if it is someone from the business function.

LX team

The LX team are a cross-functional group of people with the collective skills to create a solution that can deliver value to your internal customer and achieve the desired outcome. They are responsible for designing and developing learning experiences, enabling subject matter experts to share knowledge, curating the learning ecosystem and setting up the infrastructure. They're responsible for executing the tasks that turn the Learning Flywheel.

The requirements for the LX team can be anything from curating useful content and designing job aids to marketing your learning resources and evaluating quantitative and qualitative data. Ideally, the LX team should consist of designers, technologists, performance strategists, data analysts and marketers.

It's often impossible to get a person who can own each of those, so find people with T-shaped skills that can support across multiple disciplines. Again, the job roles don't matter as much here as the necessary skills to solve the challenge. LX team can change based on your L&D strategy and the challenge you're trying to solve.

The LX team needs to be a self-organizing team with high autonomy and accountability. They can flag any queries or blockers to the challenge owner and sprint master respectively. While the challenge owner owns the purpose and outcome, the LX team owns how you reach the outcome.

An agile approach fails when organizational hierarchy and authority are reflected in how sprint teams are organized. The sprint team should be self-organizing and must share knowledge horizontally. The Lean Learning sprint is essentially a collaborative problem-solving process that works better with synergy and strong relationships between the people involved.

By emphasizing strong collaboration, enhanced transparency and iterative feedback, we can create a learning product that solves the problem and builds an engaged and empowered sprint team that consistently achieves key outcomes.

How to run a Lean Learning sprint

The Lean Learning sprint helps you bring the key stages of Lean Learning together and implement them in two-week increments.

Stage 1: Choose your strategy

To ensure you're identifying and solving business challenges that are stopping your organization from achieving its goals in a timely manner, it's essential to regularly be conducting customer discovery interviews across the organization (see Chapter 3). The data you gather from the discovery process will give you an idea

FIGURE 11.1 The Lean Learning sprint

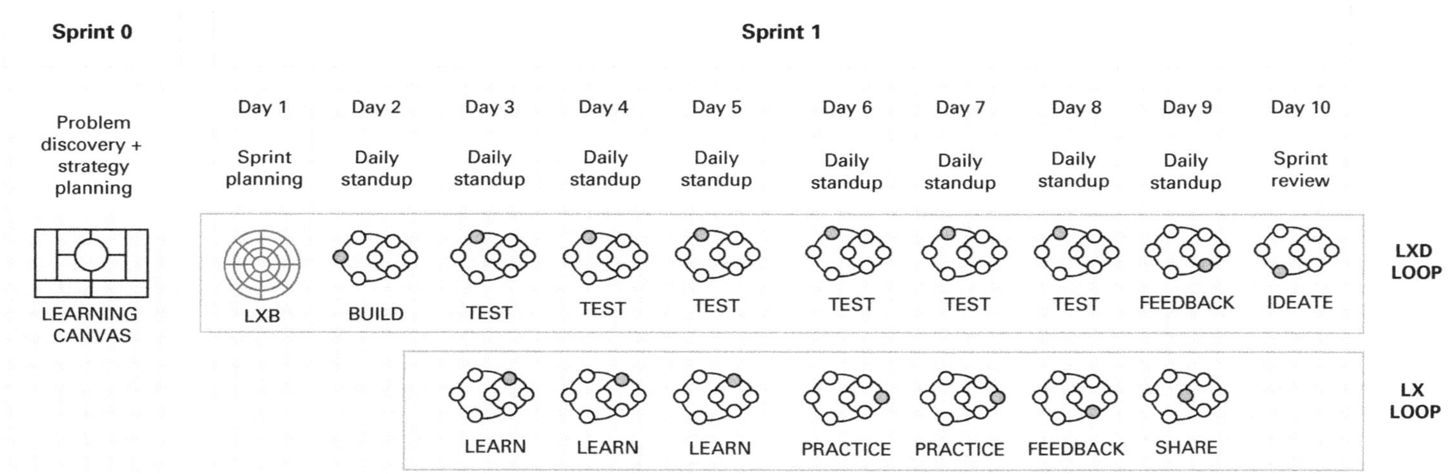

Sprint 0

Problem discovery + strategy planning

LEARNING CANVAS

Sprint 1

	Day 1	Day 2	Day 3	Day 4	Day 5	Day 6	Day 7	Day 8	Day 9	Day 10
	Sprint planning	Daily standup	Daily standup	Daily standup	Daily standup	Daily standup	Daily standup	Daily standup	Daily standup	Sprint review
LXD LOOP	LXB	BUILD	TEST	TEST	TEST	TEST	TEST	TEST	FEEDBACK	IDEATE
LX LOOP			LEARN	LEARN	LEARN	PRACTICE	PRACTICE	FEEDBACK	SHARE	

of the problems that will have the biggest impact on the business when solved.

SPRINT ZERO

Based on the problems you choose to tackle, you assemble the appropriate sprint team. With the team members in place, you start with Sprint Zero. Sprint Zero can also be two to four weeks in length. It should be lighter than subsequent sprints; however, just like normal Lean Learning sprints, you should have defined deliverables that are expected to be done. Consider this your setup phase before you start turning your Learning Flywheel.

The goal of Sprint Zero is to frame the problem and scope out the learning strategies using the Learning Canvas (see Chapter 4) for the business challenges you've identified. Remember, the Learning Canvas captures your hypothesis, and this is what you'll start testing from Sprint 1. Everyone involved in completing the Learning Canvas must be aware that the learning strategies can change through testing and learning what works and doesn't.

By the end of Sprint Zero, you'll likely end up with a backlog of completed Learning Canvases for more problems than you have the capacity to work on. That's completely normal. Focus and prioritization are critical to ensure you're working on the right things rather than working a lot. The more things you try to do simultaneously, the slower you will move.

THE VALUE VS EFFORT MATRIX

The challenge owner and sprint master should collaborate with business stakeholders to prioritize the Learning Canvases that need to be implemented first. A simple 2x2 value vs effort matrix (see Figure 11.2) can facilitate healthy discussions amongst stakeholders on what they believe value and effort mean, which can quickly help find strategic alignment. It's an easy and quick way to prioritize because it doesn't involve any complex formulas or significant steps.

Choose one to three Learning Canvases to action in the sprint from your backlog. When you first start running Lean Learning sprints, it's better to focus on one Learning Canvas because the

FIGURE 11.2 Value vs effort matrix

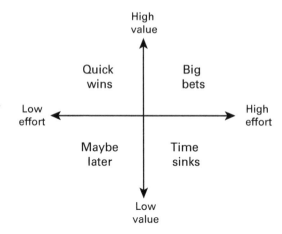

process is new to your team, and you don't want to overwhelm them. Remember, behaviour change is complex, so it's better to start small and build momentum rather than going big and prematurely dismissing a better way of doing things.

SETUP FOR SUCCESS

In Sprint Zero, the sprint team will decide the length of the subsequent sprints and consider other planning factors based on the learning strategies you have selected to test and get them in place.

For example, who are the experts we need to work with? How can we connect with our target audience? Who can you recruit to test your learning experiences? How will you get the team together for the sprint meetings? What tools and infrastructure do we need to manage our sprints and execute this learning strategy? Are there any upcoming holidays we need to be aware of that can be blockers?

Later in the chapter, we'll cover the meetings cadence in subsequent sprints. You should use the same format as the meetings in Sprint Zero, so use it as an opportunity to upskill your team in agile and lean ways of working through practice. The consistency helps build a rhythm within the team that will persist through subsequent sprints, each following the same pattern.

With all of this in place, you are all set to start your first Lean Learning sprint.

Stage 2: Map Your learning experience

The first day of Sprint 1 combines the 'ideate' step from the Learning Flywheel and sprint planning. You can split these across two workshops.

IDEA MAPPING

The idea mapping workshop should occur in the morning and should not take more than 90 minutes. The workshop's goal is to map out how you'll turn your chosen learning strategy into learning experiences.

Ideate   Using the Learning Experience Bullseye Framework (LXB) (see Chapter 9), the SM can guide the team through the discussion. The SM should start the session by introducing how the LXB works and explaining the importance of the four rights: right learning resource, right person, right moment and right impact.

Following the introduction, the SM gives everyone 5–10 minutes to jot down their ideas on sticky notes and add them to a pin-up of the LXB template, or you can do this virtually using the online template with a digital whiteboard tool.

Each idea should be made up of four sticky notes covering the four rights of the learning experience. The person suggesting the idea should add their initials and use alpha-numerals to identify which sticky notes are connected. For example, 'NS A1, NS A2...' then for the next idea 'NS B1, NS B2...'.

The SM will then read out the ideas to avoid people spending too much time explaining their own ideas. However, after they have read out the idea the SM can ask the person who wrote it if they missed anything important. Getting people to add their ideas before hearing the thoughts of others ensures everyone contributes and helps avoid any groupthink and peer influence.

Highlight ideas   There isn't enough time to discuss the merits of all the ideas that get added to the LXB, so to highlight the ideas that stand out visually, you can use 'dotmocracy'. Give each sprint team member eight dot stickers each (or can be other shaped stickers too if you want. Go wild!).

Then invite them to the LXB pin-up and give them another 5–10 minutes to add the stickers to the sticky notes with their favourite ideas. They can add the eight stickers to highlight two full learning experiences they like or use them to pick out parts of ideas they want instead of whole learning experiences. This process will help keep further discussions more focused.

Gather feedback   Now it's time to discuss the merits of the high-lighted ideas. This segment should take about 40 minutes. It's vital during this segment for the SM to facilitate effective feedback that helps expand on what is possible, rather than simply a discussion that points out problems. A useful technique to facilitate better discussions about ideas is a concept used by Pixar studios called 'plussing' (Hirsch, 2017).

When Pixar's creators get together to review a day's work, they are expected to give each other feedback to improve the work. However, there is an important rule: participants can't point out a problem without proposing an alternative, saying 'What if?' to a problem. Plussing creates an environment where you collaboratively build on ideas rather than randomly shutting down ideas completely.

So when the creative director for Pixar's upcoming *Toy Story 4* doesn't like how Woody's eyes roll from frame to frame, he won't just toss the sketch. Instead, he'll 'plus' it by asking the story artist, 'I like the way you drew Woody's eyes. What if they rolled left?' While that might seem semantic, the feedback effect is significant. Rather than reject ideas entirely, Pixar creates an additive approach to sharing feedback.

During discussions, the SM should look out for two risks:

1 **Going over time.** People love to talk about ideas, and often discussions can go into a level of detail that is unnecessary at this point in the process so it's important to get the team back on track. Remind the group that there is no guarantee any of the suggested ideas will work, and the only way to find out is to start testing. Too much time spent discussing now doesn't change that.

2 **Idea attachment.** People love their own ideas but they get too attached to them. If you find people getting defensive during the discussions, that's often a telltale sign that they're too attached. The SM can tackle this by setting the precedence that people have to explain the rationale behind their ideas and suggestions. And remember, someone's seniority is not a rationale.

By the end of the first hour, you'll have various ideas mapped to your LXB. You may have removed some ideas. You now have an idea of how your learning strategy might look as learning experiences.

Just enough research With your ideas mapped, now you use the final 30 minutes to make a list of items that need to be researched before prioritizing and defining your Minimum Valuable Learning (MVL) based on impact, confidence and effort using the ICE approach (see Chapter 9). For example, if the idea involves curating short videos, where would you get them from? Or if you're thinking of offering one-to-one virtual coaching, who will provide this and what is the cost?

The SM is responsible for delegating the tasks to each team member and communicating that the research needs to be completed by the afternoon workshop at the end of the day. This might sound like a really short turnaround time, but that is intentional. You don't want people to procrastinate on research. At this moment, you need just enough information to validate whether it's worth spending any further time working on a particular idea.

SPRINT PLANNING

It's best to schedule the second workshop late in the afternoon to give the team most of the day to research the variables flagged in the morning session. This session should also not take any longer than 90 minutes.

Prioritization In the first half of this session, you will score the different ideas for the learning experiences using the ICE approach. As you work through the scoring, team members can share what they learned from their research, i.e. costs, availability, complexity, etc.

Again, it's the SM's role to keep people on track and ensure discussions don't go off on a tangent.

With the scores in place, you will end up in one of two scenarios. Either you have a clear winner, or you'll have multiple ideas with the same ICE score. In the case of the latter, the challenge owner will decide which idea to pursue as the MVL. This avoids wasting time in endless discussions and helps the team move forward.

Backlog to sprint   The goal of your sprint is to test whether your MVL will move you towards your desired outcome. In the second half of the session, you create a sprint backlog. The sprint backlog is a to-do list of what needs to be done to start testing your MVL. Do you need to find coaches? Do you need to create job aids and upload them to your learning platform? What marketing do you need to create to make people aware of the new learning resources? We'll go into the last one in detail in the next chapter.

An effective way to manage your tasks is using a kanban board (see Figure 11.3). You can create one with most project management tools such as Trello and ClickUp. The kanban board will have the following three columns – 'To do', 'In progress', and 'Done' – so you can easily track the progress of each task. Ensure each task you add has a clear definition of what 'done' looks like and that you're not adding tasks that will take longer than a sprint to complete.

The SM is responsible for assigning each task to the relevant team member. Using labels, they can add which step in the Learning Flywheel the task refers to, e.g. if you're filming a video, label it 'build', and if you're interviewing learners, then label it 'feedback'. Keep things transparent by sharing the kanban board with everyone in the team. It's essential to add any changes or new information related to a task to the board, so you have a single source of truth for the sprint.

At the end of day one of your Lean Learning sprint, you should have defined your MVL and created a sprint backlog of tasks to get done. Sprint planning is a collaborative effort. The SM facilitates the meeting, the CO clarifies the details of the sprint backlog items and their respective acceptance criteria, and the LX team define the work and effort necessary to meet their sprint commitment.

FIGURE 11.3 Sprint kanban board

TO DO 3

Sprint 1
Run practice simulation

practice   test

Sprint 1
Get performance baseline

feedback

Sprint 1
Schedule feedback interviews

feedback

+ NEW TASK

IN PROGRESS 2

Sprint 1
Shoot expert videos

build

Sprint 1
Find test learners

feedback

+ NEW TASK

COMPLETE 2

Sprint 1
Create live class

build

Sprint 1
Setup learning channels in HowNow

build

Stage 3: Testing your MVL

Now you can start testing your MVL by going through the steps of the Learning Flywheel. The team should start picking up their tasks from the kanban board and updating the status accordingly. Any blockers that arise should be flagged to the SM. For any tasks that come up as the team progress through the flywheel, the SM should add to the sprint backlog and assign it to someone in the team.

Quite often, L&D teams that have a history of creating a lot of content fall back into old habits and spend too much of their time trying to create 'perfect' content. If there is such a thing as perfect content, it's content that gets you to learning-challenge fit and requires more than just the 'build' step. As your first sprint is your first turn of the Learning Flywheel, you have the most unknowns and assumptions. For that reason, it's better to spend less time on the build because there's a higher chance what your building could go to waste.

So in your first sprint, spend no more than one day to 'build' and then in later sprints, you can push that to two days maximum. And remember, the 'build' step is not about creating lots of your own content. It's about leveraging your learning ecosystem to build a learning experience that you can make available to your target audience as quickly as possible to start gathering feedback.

DAILY STANDUPS

Daily standups are quick 15-minute calls that take place first thing in the morning, where the sprint team flag any blockers to getting their tasks done. The SM will run the meeting, with each team member sharing the following:

- What did they get done yesterday?
- What will they do today?
- Are there any blockers stopping them from getting their work done?

The SM, with the help of the other team members, will work to remove those blockers so the team can get the task done and move forward. For example, this might require getting the right stakeholders involved as quickly as possible or getting access to the required data to complete a task.

Running daily standups keeps the team on the same page and encourages proactive communication. Teams can ensure a consistent flow of information, so no one says, 'Oh, I didn't know that was happening', or 'Sorry, I didn't know I was supposed to have this done yet'. These meetings are brief by design and play a big role in running the sprint effectively.

Schedule a recurring calendar invite to set the expectation for the same time and place. You can do the meeting in person, literally standing up, so people know it will be a quick meeting and they don't need to get too comfortable. Alternatively, you can host it virtually, with the SM sharing their screen with the kanban board.

PREPARE FOR TESTING

As you go through the Learning Experience Design loop from the Learning Flywheel within the first few days of the sprint, think ahead of things you need for user testing. You should already know your test users from Sprint Zero, but make sure you complete recruiting people to test your learning experience in the first week of the sprint.

You don't need too many people to test. According to research by Nielsen Norman Group, you can discover 85 per cent of usability problems from just five test participants and 100 per cent of problems with at least 15 users (Nielsen, 2000). Just ask them qualifier questions to ensure they match your target audience and experience the problem you're trying to solve. Confirm they will be available to test the learning experiences during the sprint.

Gathering unbiased feedback from your learners and stakeholders is critical for determining whether the challenge has been met and you have had the desired impact. Create a feedback board to capture all of your data in one place, so it's easier to identify recurring topics and share findings with the whole team.

Stage 4: Evaluate your strategy

On the last day of your sprint, it's time to evaluate what and how you've done. This can either be done in one combined workshop or spread across two workshops on the same day.

SPRINT REVIEW

This is the penultimate session in the sprint, and it involves the sprint team, key stakeholders and partners collectively reviewing the progress they made in the sprint. However, the focus is on progress from an outcome perspective rather than how many planned tasks were completed. You should allocate 90 minutes for the session.

The CO should prepare to present the feedback data from the sprint. The raw data should already be available for everyone on the feedback board, so the focus here should be on insights. This session enables the feedback to turn the Learning Flywheel again. If you've not tested your MVL by this point in the sprint, it's impossible to start the feedback loop.

The insights should be organized to demonstrate the parts of the learning experience that helped move you towards your desired outcome and those that didn't – and what you can learn from them, respectively. For example, did a learning resource get high engagement but poor qualitative feedback about its usefulness? This might validate the need and effectiveness of marketing but suggest the learning resource doesn't deliver the required value. The CO's insights should form the foundation for further discussion about what could be changed.

The expectation in the session isn't to define new learning experiences but to identify the parts of the learning experience and learning strategy that need a new hypothesis. It's possible that the feedback data doesn't show movement in the metric you're using to track outcome after one sprint. In that case, the CO should use the available data to build the impact narrative.

For example, you might have qualitative feedback from your test users about how the learning experience has (or hasn't) influenced their performance and quantitative metrics about learning engagement. The SM should capture these insights and action items that arise from the discussion, as they will be required to facilitate the 'idea mapping' session on day one of the next sprint.

SPRINT RETROSPECTIVE

The retrospective is the last meeting in the sprint, and it only requires the sprint team. It's a post-mortem on the sprint facilitated by the SM to identify how to improve the way the sprint team work together. This session is an opportunity to review the team's performance rather than the performance of the learning experience.

The SM can structure the session around a three-question agenda:

1 How successful was the sprint? Rate by selecting a number from 1–10 (10 meaning very successful) and explain why.

2 What went well? Celebrate some wins!

3 How could you improve the way you work?

For each question, everyone should capture their answers on sticky notes. One sticky note for each thought. Did you manage to curate helpful resources faster? Was it challenging to work with the experts? Get the sprint team to put it down on a sticky note. It's worth making sure everyone knows the format of the sprint retrospective, and that they're made aware that they will need to contribute so they can come prepared.

The purpose of the session is to push the team to evaluate their performance honestly rather than glossing over errors and overhyping success. The retrospective is also a great opportunity for everyone in the team to voice their feedback. Positive or negative, all fair and reasonable feedback should be considered. Over time, this process will become a habit that helps push the team toward continuous improvement.

And that's it. You've completed your first sprint. You'll be starting all over again with your next sprint, but this time with more information. The first few sprints you run will feel intense because you're fundamentally changing how your team works together to solve business challenges using learning.

Many times, you can go from 'this is brilliant' to 'this won't work' in minutes, which is an uncomfortable feeling. This is a part of the process, and it's important to reinforce to the team that if they trust it, it will work. It helps to congratulate, thank and applaud the team for their work and participation. Have a team social at the end of each sprint to break from sprint chat and develop relationships between team members.

Lean Learning sprints can help you implement the Learning Flywheel and generate remarkable impact quickly without wasting resources. The sprint framework keeps you focused on the outcome rather than output. Your Learning Flywheel gains momentum with every sprint and accelerates how quickly you can achieve Learning-Challenge Fit.

What next?

Once you achieve learning-challenge fit, you're ready to scale your learning experience to all the people who need it. But how do you get their attention in a world where the competition for people's attention is fierce? The answer is marketing.

In the next chapter, you'll learn how to think like a marketer and build a marketing funnel that scales your impact.

References

Hirsch, J (2017) Pixar's secret for giving feedback (communication), *LeadX*, 20 June, https://leadx.org/articles/pixar/ (archived at https://perma.cc/98PS-K6MR)

Johnson, P (2012) NPR adopts Agile-like method for program development, *Computer World*, 15 August, https://www.computerworld.com/article/2505876/npr-adopts-agile-like-method-for-program-development.html (archived at https://perma.cc/LHG6-6NDR)

Knapp, J (2016) *Sprint: How to solve big problems and test new ideas in just five days*, Simon and Schuster

Nielsen, J (2000) Why you only need to test with 5 users, Nielsen Norman Group, 18 March, https://www.nngroup.com/articles/why-you-only-need-to-test-with-5-users/ (archived at https://perma.cc/K4UA-25CE)

Sutherland, JJ (2014) *Scrum: The art of doing twice the work in half the time*, Currency

12

Scale your learning impact with marketing

Don't count the people that you reach, reach the people who count.

DAVID OGILVY, FOUNDER OF OGILVY & MATHER

In 2014, five guys got together to disrupt the mattresses industry. Their idea was to sell mattresses directly to customers online, with no brick-and-mortar stores, no salespeople, and no touching the mattress before you buy it. Today, their company, Casper, is worth over $1 billion and serves over a million customers. How did a mattress company grow so fast?

Not only did Casper reinvent the way people bought mattresses, but they successfully created a brand that stood out in an otherwise sleepy industry. They created an instantly memorable visual identity that is wholly modern, tongue in cheek and evoked convenience and ease. Their ad campaigns, seen on billboards, subway platforms and television, struck a consistently friendly and inclusive tone.

Casper used content marketing to garner trust and build the authority necessary to position their brand as the experts in the space. Whether you want information on relaxation techniques, getting more sleep, or measuring your room for the best bed size, Casper have the content to fill the needs of their customers.

They financially incentivized their customers to share their stories and then used social media to amplify their positive experiences.

Regardless of how you came across their content, Casper did a brilliant job, including a strong call to action and links back to their product pages to boost conversion on their organic traffic (Krans, 2019).

Casper is one of the most successful in a class of startups turning mundane, unloved consumer products like beds, toothbrushes, suitcases, water bottles and vitamins into something exciting and fun. What's the moral of the story? There's no such thing as a boring product, just boring marketing. So if you can market a mattress, why can't we market the thing that will help people perform better and solve business challenges – learning?

Organizations often fail to drive business impact with learning because the internal customers don't 'buy' what L&D is selling. That is a marketing gap, not a learning one. Marketing can help build a culture of continuous learning by creating a consistent demand for it. Today the competition for people's attention and engagement is fierce, and L&D need to think like marketers to have a real impact on the business.

In this chapter, we'll look at how we can use the marketing tactics successfully implemented by startups with few resources to disrupt competitive markets, to deliver learning that connects with our internal customers.

How the L&D marketing funnel works

Why do some people end up engaging with learning resources while some don't? This question is not much different from marketers trying to understand why some people buy and others don't. To answer both of these questions, we need to understand the buyer's journey – the process they go through to decide if they're going to commit their time, effort and/or money. This is where the marketing funnel comes in.

What is a marketing funnel?

A marketing funnel outlines the journey taken by a prospective customer from the moment they learn about your product or service until they sign up or buy. The idea is that, like a funnel, marketers start by casting a broad net to capture as many leads as possible, but the number of prospective customers lessens as they move down each stage of the funnel.

Marketing funnels are a helpful tool for understanding the buyer's needs at each step in the journey. Marketers can use this insight to understand when and why prospects drop off before purchasing and optimize their tactics to get them to the next stage in the buying process.

Even if you've never sat down to create a marketing funnel formally, you probably already have a funnel without knowing it. And you've definitely been in someone else's funnel. For example, a marketing funnel can be if you hear about a brand for the first time through the content on their blog, then you sign up to their newsletter, and then you end up buying their product.

The stages of the L&D marketing funnel

While the journey through the L&D marketing funnel can vary from person to person, the primary focus is ultimately on the singular journey from vague awareness to confirmed commitment. An employee's relationship with L&D can be captured using the four stages of the A2R2 marketing funnel. At each stage of this funnel, L&D can choose from a range of marketing tactics to move the employee on to the next.

STAGE 1: AWARENESS

Recognizing there is a problem and you need a solution is the first step in the decision-making process. People will not engage with L&D if they're not aware of a problem that needs solving or don't know what solutions are on offer.

In the awareness stage, the employee needs to be made aware of the business problems and possible solutions. At this stage, to attract your internal customers, it is about educating them as quickly as possible about the challenges and then informing them of how we can help solve them.

Here are a few marketing tactics to create awareness:

- building a learning brand
- social media
- influencer marketing
- search engine optimization

STAGE 2: ACTIVATION

In the activation stage, the goal is to convince your internal customer that a learning experience can solve their problem and get them to commit to it. This stage marks the start of the learning experience loop. It's when they open a course, join a knowledge-sharing community, book onto a live class.

Here are a few marketing tactics to drive activation:

- search engine optimization
- product positioning
- social proof
- calls to action

STAGE 3: RETENTION

The journey isn't over once they start engaging with the learning experience. To solve your business challenge, you need to keep learners engaged until you drive the performance improvement. In the retention stage, the focus is on keeping the learner engaged with the learning experiences until they see a measurable performance improvement.

You need to retain the employee to ensure they practise the knowledge they acquire, give and receive feedback, and share what they are learning. The retention stage ensures they keep coming back to reinforce the learning.

Marketing tactics to retain learners include:

- nudge marketing
- notifications

STAGE 4: REFERRAL

The referral stage of the marketing funnel refers to the moment customers become fans of your learning brand. They turn into advocates and start sharing what they learn and recommend it to others.

Marketing tactics to enable referrals include:

- influencer marketing
- social proof

Each marketing tactic can help you move the learner through each marketing funnel stage. Let's look at how you can put each tactic into action within your organization.

Building a learning brand

Apple sells technology products, like many other companies, but why do customers queue up around the block for a chance to get one of their latest products? The answer is the same as why there was a low demand for electric cars, yet there was a high demand for Teslas. It's the brand. The power of a brand can generate demand, increase prices, and drive us to pay to wear it like a walking billboard.

Most people mistake brand building for pretty logos and flashy ads. It's a lot more than that. Your brand is the sum of people's interactions with your business, all designed to shape how they think and feel about you. It should tell the story of why your company exists and how you add value to the world around you. Logos and adverts are just a part of that story. As an organization, you probably spend a lot of time, energy and money on building your external brand, but what about building your learning brand for internal customers?

Whether you like it or not, L&D within your organization has a brand. If you're not aware of it or deliberately shaping it, then there's a chance it might not be a good one. There's a risk that people perceive L&D as just course providers and deadline chasers rather than problem solvers and performance improvers. Even worse, employees might not even know L&D exists in the organization and be completely unaware of the learning resources and tools on offer; therefore, they never think of L&D as a possible solution.

The L&D team should own the process of building your organization's learning brand, but that's not to say only they should be involved – quite the contrary. The making of the learning brand is an excellent opportunity to work across the organization, to understand what people expect from the L&D team and how they currently perceive what you do. Your marketing team is also an obvious collaborator to help you execute your brand vision.

So what should a good learning brand include? Here are five elements to think about.

Who is it for?

Your learning brand is for your internal customers, but who are they? What motivates them? Who do they trust? Are they early adopters? Why would they need L&D? Knowing your internal customers will help you decide every aspect of your brand strategy and build a learning brand that genuinely connects with employees.

Your people should be at the heart of your learning brand because they'll be the ones to ultimately determine its success. Placing them on the back burner is where most people go wrong when building their brand.

Why does it exist?

In Simon Sinek's now-famous TED talk, 'How Great Leaders Inspire Action', he explains that people are motivated to buy into a product, service, movement or idea only when they understand the 'why' behind it (Sinek, 2009). The 'why' is the reason you get up every morning and come to work. What problem do you solve for people? Why should they care? Your customer wants to know who you are, what you stand for, and how you're going to make their life better or easier.

In many organizations, L&D talk about WHAT they do and HOW they do it but tend not to communicate the WHY effectively. According to Sinek, 'people don't buy WHAT you do; they buy WHY you do it' because it creates a shared belief that they can identify with. When your WHY matches their WHY, people are motivated to take action.

So WHY do we need workplace learning? To enable people to be successful at what they do. This shared belief will motivate organizations to invest and employees to engage in workplace learning. For organizations, if their people are successful at what they do, it means they're solving business challenges. For the employees, if they're successful at what they do, they're happier, more fulfilled, and progress further in their career. It's a WHY that both the organization and workforce can identify with.

There are three elements you can use to communicate this WHY in a way that captures what success looks like for your people and your organization:

BRAND MISSION

A good brand mission brings together the community, and the alignment helps build a deep bond. For example, lifestyle brand Brit + Co's mission is to 'ignite the creative spark in women'. A clear and compelling statement that draws you into the community.

Craft a learning brand mission that builds on your organization's mission statement and communicates why people should care. You can use this simple formula to write your brand mission statement:

Our mission is to (what you do) by (how you do it) for (who you serve) to (the value you deliver).

BRAND VALUES

Brand values are the core beliefs that you, as an L&D team, stand for. They act as guiding principles that shape your actions, behaviours and decision-making process. Brand values play an important role in fostering deeper connections that turn one-time learners into lifelong learning advocates.

Here are examples of brand values that might work for your learning brand:

- Relentless Curiosity
- Collectively Genius

- Go Further, Faster
- Unleash Potential
- Accomplish Together
- Build the Future
- Break the Mould

Take your time while discovering your brand values and dig deep to ensure the values you choose really get to the heart of your learning brand.

BRAND STORY

A brand story communicates your values. It's a narrative that evokes emotions and draws people in to connect with your learning brand. The critical thing to remember is your learning brand is not the hero of that story. Your people are. To connect with employees, your brand story must communicate how your learning brand will help them improve their life.

Approach your brand story as if you are responding to someone at a party who asks you what you do. You wouldn't reel off your mission statement. You'd tell them a story in your own words. What's the problem you're solving and why? Why does it get you out of bed? You would say it all in your own words.

For example, you'll find the brand story for social enterprise Toms Shoes on their website. It reads that the founder Blake Mycoskie 'witnessed the hardships faced by children growing up without shoes' while travelling in Argentina in 2006. 'Wanting to help, he created Toms Shoes, a company that would match every pair of shoes purchased with a new pair of shoes for a child in need' (Toms, nd). The power of their story was able to help the brand stand out in an otherwise crowded market.

What's your brand name?

You can create a brand name that captures your vision with a better understanding of who your brand is for and why it exists. The name should be memorable, uncomplicated and easily associated with what you offer your customers. You want the sound to convey the right emotions or ideas to your audience.

There are a few different approaches you can take:

- **Functional names.** These are descriptive names that state what you do. They're clear, concise and easy to remember – for example, ACME University, ACME Academy or ACME Learning Hub.
- **Emotive names.** These are names designed to evoke an emotional response based on how the customer feels when they engage with your brand – for example, 'Catalyst', 'Bloom at ACME' or 'Excel at Work'.
- **Playful names.** These names can be made-up words, rhyming words, slang, or reference to a mascot. They tend not to connect with what you do directly, but they're fun, easy to remember and stand out – for example, Mind Jam, Work in Progress or Clever Cows.
- **Metaphor names.** These names can express an idea by making you think of another image that your target audience can identify with and be a great starting point for a brand voice – for example, Thunderbolt (speed, power), Unicorns (wonder, success), or Athena (goddess of wisdom).

When deciding on your learning brand name, think about the first impression you want to make. Are you inspiring and pioneering? Or a fun and accessible sidekick? The name will likely be the most used part of your brand identity. You can further support the brand name with a catchy slogan. These few words capture what you do and help make a solid first impression. For example, your slogan can be literal: ACME Academy, 'Smarter, Together'; or stake a claim: Thunderbolt, 'Fastest Learners Win'.

What's your brand identity?

The brand identity is how your audience will see you. It's your visual identity, and it consists of logo, brand colours, fonts and imagery. The logo is likely to be seen the most and the first thing people notice about your learning brand. Keep it simple and instantly recognizable. Just take a look at the logo of the most valuable brand in the world (Statista, 2021): it's an apple with a bite taken out of it.

Here are a few things to consider when designing your logo:

- Will the logo work in all the places you'll need to use it?
- Does it reflect your organizational culture?
- Does the logo capture what you do?
- How does the logo look in different sizes?

The brand colours, fonts and imagery can be based on your organization's visual guidelines or create a unique look to your learning brand. Create a document that sets out the visual guidelines for the L&D team to use in their marketing material across the different channels they use. The brand identity represents the organization's L&D team and can be extended to the broader organization if you have academies or learning hubs for each department.

However, it's important not to force visual guidelines upon internal experts sharing knowledge and moderating communities, as this will cause unnecessary friction. Companies make the mistake of trying to control every aspect of all learning content that goes out, which is counterproductive as it slows down the knowledge-sharing process.

What's your tone of voice?

Put your hand up if your parent has ever said, 'don't use that tone of voice with me'. You probably didn't like it as a kid, but it would be highly beneficial to get feedback on your tone of voice as a marketer. However, it's not as readily available. If you speak to your audience in the wrong way, you could lose them and not have any indication about the specifics of why they leave.

People buy from people, not brands, so the more you bring personality to your brand, the better you will develop meaningful connections with your customers. The tone of voice you use is an effective way to express the L&D team's personality and embody the people behind the brand.

Your tone of voice is not just how you speak, but the words you use and how you use them. For example, the personal care brand Dove has created an empowering and uplifting tone by consistently using affirmative and empathetic language such as 'feel beautiful' and 'embrace yourself' to boost its audience's self-confidence.

You might want your learning brand to come across as casual or approachable, so you might use slang, emojis and humour to do that. Or you want to be aspirational, so you might avoid negative language.

Here are things to consider when creating guidelines for your tone of voice:

- What words would you like to associate with your learning brand?
- If the brand was a person, how would you describe them?
- Will your tone of voice work in every country you operate in?
- Does it work for all the age groups in your audience?
- If you're using humour, is it suitable for your organizational culture?
- How do your audience talk to one another?

When creating the tone of voice guide, include clear examples in different contexts. For example, how would you apply it on social media? How would it affect other comms sent out from your learning brand? This helps other team members understand how to keep a uniform tone across all of your communications, so your audience gains a better sense of what your brand stands for.

Getting the tone of voice right is critical for building an emotional connection, encouraging engagement. It builds trust with your audience, which is vital if you want them to believe you can help. The tone of voice can make your brand just as memorable as your logo and brand identity. If in doubt, just read Slack's app release notes.

With these five steps, you can start building your learning brand. Keep reviewing these steps as your brand might change as your audience or needs change. Your learning brand is the heart and soul of what your

L&D team does. It is responsible for shaping how people see L&D, creating advocates and driving measurable impact in your organization.

Putting social media to work

Almost half of the world's population are on social media, and studies show that as many as 40 per cent of Internet users follow the social media accounts of their favourite brands (Chen, 2021). It's how brands share insights, engage in discussion, solicit feedback and develop a stronger relationship with their audience.

So how can you ensure your learning brand gets seen? More importantly, how can you engage and capture the right people's attention? Here are a few ways you can use social media to support the L&D marketing funnel.

Get on social media

L&D teams often spend too much time trying to get their audience to come to them rather than being more proactive and going to the audience. Most people reading this book probably have accounts on more than one social network, and it's likely the same for the people you work with. So why not create social media profiles for your learning brand so you can show up on their feed?

For example, create an Instagram account for your learning brand and share it with your audience. Got a new course out? Create an Instagram story that captures what you'll learn from it. Have you received great feedback about your learning experiences? Take a screenshot of the review and share it. Do the same across other social networks used by your audience. Don't know which ones are popular? Then ask.

There are many social media platforms to choose from, and you don't need to be on all of them. It's more critical to select the platforms that will give you the right exposure with the right audience.

For example, if your audience consists of creatives, your learning brand might lend itself to Instagram and TikTok. If you're in financial services, a platform like Twitter focused on real-time events might work better. Or you might need a mix of multiple channels to cater for a very diverse workforce.

Once your audience follows you with their accounts on their preferred social networks, you'll now show up on their feeds. Given that, on average, a user spends 144 minutes a day on social media sites (Henderson, 2020), this is a powerful tool to create awareness for your learning brand.

Tag and hashtag

Want to get someone's attention on social media? Tag them. They'll instantly receive a notification, and you will get impressions from their network – which is likely to include other colleagues. But you don't want to spam-tag people. Instead, use it as an opportunity to give someone a shout out and highlight success stories. It doesn't have to be just in posts; you can also tag people in comments to relevant posts. They'll also receive notifications and get exposed to the network.

Hashtagging helps your followers to easily know what something is about, especially if it's a part of a broader campaign. For example, for Mental Health Awareness Week, you might want to bring attention to helpful learning resources that you've curated. You can use a branded hashtag like **#wellbeingatACME** for related posts on social media. Not only does it make it easy to track the engagement you received for related posts, but it also makes it easier for people to find related content.

Share valuable content

Don't just use social media to shout about learning resources you offer. Instead, use it actually to share learning. You might be familiar with microlearning, but you could use social media to create nano-learning that adds value. For example, how-tos as 15-second

TikTok reels or Twitter Spaces to host short discussions about relevant topics.

You can natively create and share content using social media apps or use other tools to create content then use social media to distribute it. Canva is an excellent tool for design novices to leverage templates to create professional-looking content easily shared on social media. Remember, their social feed is where people see content from friends, influencers, thought leaders, and brands they're interested in, so it needs to be high-quality and authentic.

Engage your audience

It's called social media for a reason – the operative word being 'social'. Social media platforms are great for starting a conversation, interacting with your audience, and nurturing relationships. You can get a relevant discussion going by posting questions. What skill will be the most important in your industry in the next five years? Post a poll and ask your people.

Get your people involved in your marketing campaigns. For example, ask your followers to share a picture of the book that influenced their career the most, with a specific hashtag like #bestbooks. Then reshare the pictures you like the most across your social channels. The photo-taker gets attention and accolades, reinforcing their affinity for your learning brand. And you get to share authentic content that drives more engagement.

Giveaways have been a staple part of marketing strategies for decades. Why? Because people love them. Done right, you can expand your brand reach. For example, ask your followers to tag someone in the organization they consider a mentor or comment with the best piece of professional advice they've received. Pick a winner and give them a little prize.

Keep showing up

Consistency is to social media what spinach is to Popeye. You need to post consistently to keep your learning brand front of mind. But when should you post? This varies based on the social network and your audience.

Typically, B2B organizations get the most engagement during 8–9 am around the morning commute, 12–1 pm around lunch, 5–6 pm on people's way back home, and as late as 8–9 pm when people are winding down for the day. Facebook tends to see higher click-through rates towards the end of the week, while Monday to Thursday are better days to post on LinkedIn, Instagram and Twitter. Coincidence? Not really. If you think about it, people shop for business needs when working (weekdays) and personal needs when they're off work (weekends) (Kolowich Cox, 2019).

These days/times are guidelines, but if you choose to use a social media management tool like Hootsuite, Buffer or Sprout Social, you can use their data around the best times to post to plan and schedule your social content.

Social media is an excellent weapon in your arsenal. But wait, what if people copy our content and get access to our IP? Firstly, you're not going to be sharing your trade secrets on social media. The substance of what you share is unlikely to be unique to your organization, but the style will be specific to your learning brand.

What's the worst that can happen if your competitor gets inspired from your social learning brand's social content and starts copying it? This hasn't stopped the biggest brands in the world from sharing amazing content on social media, and neither should it stop you – because the upside is worth it.

Influencer marketing

China's Li Jiaqi, a live streamer widely known as the 'lipstick brother', sold $1.9 billion in goods on the first day of Alibaba's annual shopping festival, Singles' Day (Hong, 2021). This is the power of influencer marketing. But what is it? As the name suggests, influencer marketing involves partnering with people of influence to support your marketing.

Influencers don't have to be celebrities or have massive followers. They can be someone with authority, expertise or a special relationship with their audience. Even if they influence a small yet loyal audience, that can be powerful. Today, it's almost impossible to scroll through your social feeds without seeing influencer marketing in action.

From selling clothes and makeup to shaping elections, influencers drive decisions everywhere you look. The power of influencer marketing can also be used to improve communication, increase engagement and amplify change initiatives, including learning within your organization.

Choose the right influencers

The good news is every organization, whether it has 50 employees or 50,000, has influencers. But just because someone is in a position of power, it doesn't mean they have the ear of your people by default. In fact, research has found the five most influential people in a workforce can reach more than double the number of people a five-person leadership team can (Herrero, 2014).

The right internal influencers can help you get your learning brand and what you offer in front of more of the right people. Here are a few factors to consider to determine whether they're appropriate for your audience:

- **Reach:** How much of your target audience can the influencer's content reach?
- **Engagement:** How do people react to content the influencer shares?
- **Relevance:** Is the influencer known for something relevant to your target audience?
- **Experience:** How much authority does the influencer have amongst your target audience?

Sometimes your influencers might hold leadership positions such as team leaders and line managers, but this isn't necessary or always the case. They can be team members who have earned the trust and respect of their peers and have naturally become the go-to for advice and reliable information about things happening in the organization and broader industry.

You probably know some of the influencers in your organization already. You might see them regularly share knowledge on LinkedIn. They might be the first to respond to questions from colleagues in your team chat tool and proactively play the role of a bridge across different teams. Internal influencers are likely very sociable and make an effort to connect with people outside of work.

However, don't stop there because there's a good chance you've missed some of the influencers. You can find influencers by simply asking your target audience through anonymous surveys and in your customer discovery interviews. Who do they go to when they need help or advice? Get in touch with the suggested people. You can also put out a call for influencers and let them put themselves forward.

Empower your influencers

Influencers will help expand the impact of your learning strategy, but what's in it for them? To get real value for your influencer campaign, you don't want them to feel obligated to do so or as if it's an additional task. Internal influencers ultimately want to increase their exposure and engagement across the organization and be recognized for their value. It is essential to communicate to them how you'll be helping them do that.

Offer your influencers the infrastructure to amplify their message rather than taking away their autonomy and prescribing what they should say and do. The influencers must remain authentic because that's what has earned them their credibility and the trust of their audience. Give them the space to post on your learning brand's social media, to write on your company blog and platform to spread awareness of what they believe in. Make it easy and quick for them to create useful content by providing templates.

Get your influencers to follow you on your social media channels and ask them to share content that they think is relevant with their networks and peers.

Co-create content with influencers

Discuss your goals with the influencers and ask them how they think they can help. Do you want to bring attention to the new learning resources you've curated? Or share the success stories of how learning has helped solve business challenges? Based on the goals, work with your influencers to co-create content.

It could be a short reel to share on social media or a podcast interviewing your internal influencers about the impact of learning on their progress. Again, the content doesn't have to shout about your learning brand or announce the launch of a new course. For example, Google created an advert in collaboration with the founder of the online urban music platform SBTV, Jamal Edwards (Marketing Society, nd).

The advert tracks his progress from a 15-year-old school kid uploading rap videos shot on his camcorder to YouTube, to becoming a media mogul, including the Google products he used along the way. It became the second-most-viewed UK YouTube video in its year of release. Similarly, you can create inspiring content featuring the progress of your internal influencers. This could be in the form of a podcast interview or a short video shot on your phone.

Another great way to collaborate on content is by featuring internal influencers in the learning content itself. A technology company we work with at HowNow did this really well by featuring internal influencers in the GDPR course they created, resulting in one of the highest first-day uptakes we've seen.

Influencers can help communicate the importance of the problems and value of the solutions on offer in relatable terms that employees understand. They can also be your eyes and ears on the ground, giving you insights and feedback from conversations taking place at grassroots level.

Search engine optimization (SEO)

When we need to find the answer to something, our go-to behaviour is to search online. It's no different when we need to know something for work. Optimizing your learning resources for search is critical for supporting self-directed learning. After all, there's little value in putting in the effort to bring together your learning ecosystem if it's difficult for people to find what they need to start with.

Search across different platforms employs specific algorithms, and SEO makes it more likely that the most relevant learning resources appear first when someone searches. SEO can help you attract anyone with intent at a given point in time, no matter what stage of the marketing funnel they are at. It helps to bring awareness to your learning resources, match with intent to generate activation, and increase retention and referrals through credibility.

People can discover relevant learning resources, solve problems faster, and experience the value of your learning brand. SEO is a low-cost yet highly effective marketing tactic that helps your people spend less time searching and more time doing and should not be overlooked. But where do you start? With keyword research.

Keyword research

Keyword research helps you understand what your internal customers want and how they search for it. Keywords are the words and phrases your learners will use to search for a learning resource. For example, if you were looking to learn 'how to do a vlookup on Excel', the keyword is 'vlookup'. So how can you find out what keywords people will use?

Customer discovery interviews will give you an insight into how people talk about a problem. These are likely the words they'll use when searching for a solution. You can ask in the interviews if there are other ways some might describe the problem, or what they need to know to solve it. You can also use your learning platform to gather search data. For example, L&D teams use HowNow to see what the top searches are. This highlights what people are looking for and what keywords they use to describe what they're looking for.

Suppose you don't currently have a learning platform or tool to gather internal search data – not to worry. You can also use Google's free Keyword Planner tool to gather insights on how people search.

Enter the keywords from your interviews and topics related to the problem you're trying to solve into the Keyword Planner. The tool will then share data around what relevant keywords people use to search and the search volume for each keyword. This is a valuable exercise even if you do have internal search data because it can help you proactively create search-optimized content.

Optimizing content for SEO

Once you've done your keyword research, you can use those insights to optimize your learning resources to match search intent. When we use the exact keywords in our learning resources that the target audience would use when searching for them, the search engine in your learning platform will know to rank them higher as this will give people what they want.

The search engine in your learning platform will typically look for these keywords in the title, description, headings and body of the content, applying a different weightage depending on where they are used and how often. By including keywords in the right parts of the content, you can ensure the top search results are the most relevant.

More intelligent learning platforms can go a step further to support search optimization. For example, HowNow looks at other learning resources you may have linked back to within your content. The platform also automatically suggests relevant keywords you might want to use while creating content. You can also optimize the content you curate by adding your own tags and organizing them into appropriate content channels.

The keyword research data can be used to identify and close content gaps. If 70 per cent of your people are searching for 'how to sell remotely' yet you have no useful resources for that search, then it's fair to assume you should create or curate content to support that demand. You can also use it to inform how you market your learning brand and the experiences you offer. From social media posts to posters you might put up in your workplace, the keyword data informs us of the best way to write about the value we can add to the learner.

Learning resources that match the searcher's intent are likely to engage more, ultimately increasing the probability of adding value and driving impact. With your audience engaging more frequently and for longer, you can expect them to develop a stronger connection with your learning brand, earning you more trust and loyalty over time.

Product positioning

There's a lot of learning content in the world. Why should people commit time and effort to the learning resources you've created or curated? Why do your learning experiences matter to your audience? Why should your internal customer care about the product you're offering? Product positioning helps you communicate this to your audience.

According to April Dunford, author of *Obviously Awesome* (2019), positioning is like context setting for the product. It helps orient customers about how your product can add value to them.

Think of it as the opening scene of a movie. When Steven Spielberg's *Jurassic Park* opens with the velociraptor killing an InGen employee while still confined to its cage, it sets the context for the danger posed by dinosaurs from the beginning. Once we have established some context, we can settle in and pay attention to the story's finer details.

When done right, positioning can provide your learners with valid assumptions about the learning and development on offer. Positioning will drive the rest of your marketing plan, from the titles and descriptions you use for your resources to content you share on social media. As a result, positioning makes it easier for employees to commit to learning experiences.

The positioning of your learning experiences should include:

- What problem are you going to solve?
- How will this learning experience solve this problem?
- What is the benefit of solving this problem?
- Who are you solving this problem for?
- How will we know once we've solved this problem?

FIGURE 12.1 Learning Canvas

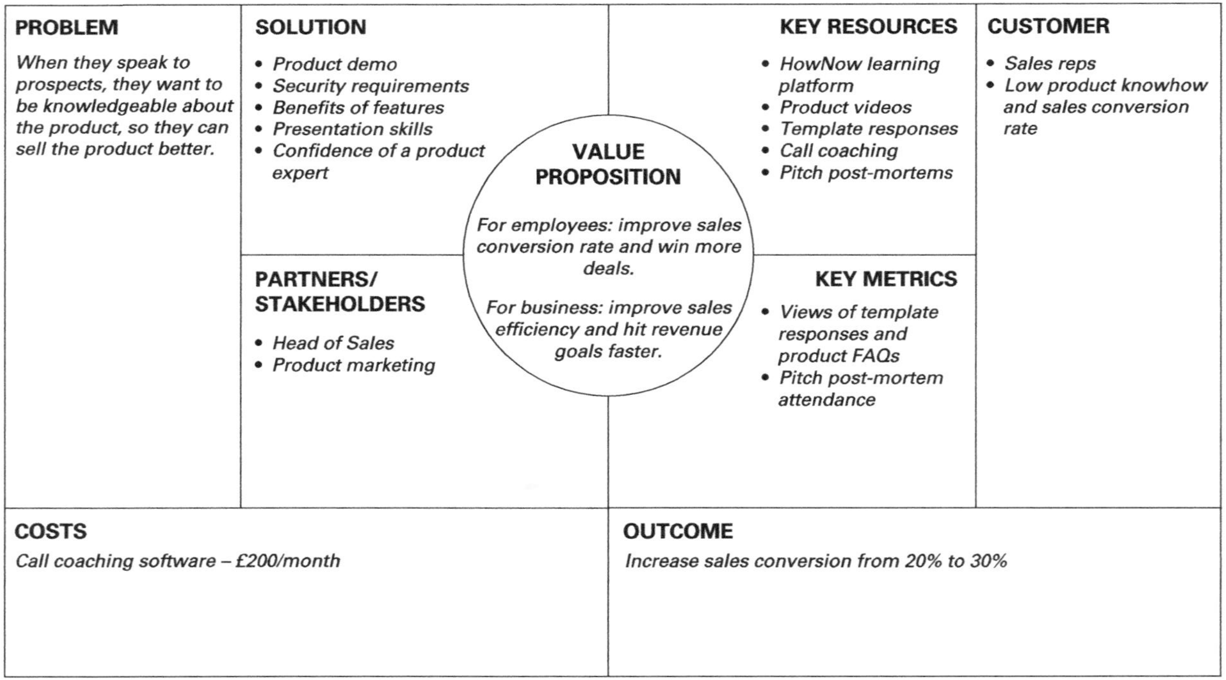

PROBLEM	SOLUTION		KEY RESOURCES	CUSTOMER
When they speak to prospects, they want to be knowledgeable about the product, so they can sell the product better.	• Product demo • Security requirements • Benefits of features • Presentation skills • Confidence of a product expert	**VALUE PROPOSITION** For employees: improve sales conversion rate and win more deals. For business: improve sales efficiency and hit revenue goals faster.	• HowNow learning platform • Product videos • Template responses • Call coaching • Pitch post-mortems	• Sales reps • Low product knowhow and sales conversion rate
	PARTNERS/ STAKEHOLDERS • Head of Sales • Product marketing		**KEY METRICS** • Views of template responses and product FAQs • Pitch post-mortem attendance	

COSTS	OUTCOME
Call coaching software – £200/month	Increase sales conversion from 20% to 30%

All of these questions are answered in your Learning Canvas so you can use the blocks to create a narrative that helps you position your learning experiences. For example, in Figure 12.1 you'll see a completed Learning Canvas that captures FiveADay.com's learning strategy. Here's how it can be converted as a narrative to position the learning experience:

> *If you're a sales rep struggling to win more deals, call coaching sessions can help you improve your ability to have knowledgeable conversations with potential customers by giving you personalized feedback on your calls. People like to buy from experts, so you can increase your win rate and hit the sales target with better product knowledge.*

This narrative helps position the learning resource for the target audience. It effectively and quickly sets the scene so the employee can quickly decide whether to commit any further time and energy.

Calls to action (CTAs)

You can have an awesome logo, stunning graphics and engaging copy, but what good is all that if it doesn't drive action? To turn your marketing into an action-inducing, learning-driving machine, you need compelling calls to action (CTAs). This is what turns passive browsers into active learners.

A study found that marketing emails that contained a powerful, single call to action got 371 per cent more clicks than those without (Protocol 80, 2020). But that doesn't mean sticking in a bold text or a big button is enough to compel people to take action.

Here are a few ways to make your CTAs more effective:

- Use value-focused words and phrases such as 'Become a better speaker' or 'Get the skills you need', rather than 'open course' and 'learn more'.

- Position them logically at the point in your marketing where someone is likely to make a decision – for example, at the end of a 'success story' video or next to the benefits of a course on its landing page.

- Create FOMO (Fear Of Missing Out) by showing social proof of others who have used the learning resource, displaying countdown timers or decreasing availability for live events.

- Make them stand out by using contrasting colours and distinctive shapes and by keeping it to only one CTA so your target audience doesn't experience a choice paradox.

CTAs may be small, but they're compelling. By giving a little attention to CTAs, you can turn the attention you get into action.

Nudge marketing

In the 1990s, a cleaning manager at Schiphol Airport wanted to cut down on mess around the public urinals. The situation was getting out of hand and they needed a way to get people to aim better. Apparently, the drain wasn't enough of a target to aim for: people needed something else. So, the cleaning manager gave it to them. The airport added small etchings of flies to the urinals. This simple tactic resulted in an incredible 80 per cent less mess and much happier cleaning staff. This is what's known as a nudge.

In their book *Nudge*, Nobel Prize-winner Richard Thaler and Harvard professor Cass Sunstein (2009) define the term as 'any aspect of the choice architecture that predictably alters people's behaviour without forbidding any options or significantly changing their economic incentives. To count as a nudge, the intervention must be easy and cheap to avoid.' In other words, nudging is the process of designing subtle cues for people to perform the desired behaviour – like the flies in the urinal (Ingraham, 2017).

Why do nudges work? Humans use heuristics to help make better decisions. These are essentially shortcuts that our efficiency-driven brains take to help make decisions as automated as possible. Nudges enable us to form those connections faster. In fact, nudges are so powerful that the US and UK Governments had dedicated 'Nudge Units' to encourage people to make better social choices (Shah et al, 2019).

Nudge marketing involves using nudges to encourage customers to perform specific actions. If you've ever bought B2B software, you might be familiar with the pricing page that compares three different subscriptions with one labelled 'Most Popular'. That label is an example of nudge marketing in action. Let's look at ways to implement nudge marketing to drive more activation and retention.

Social proofs

Imagine you're shopping for a new desk. You've found two that you love, based on the pictures alone. One has over 300 reviews with an average rating of 4.7 stars. The second has 40 reviews and a 2-star rating. Which one would you buy? You're likely attracted to the desk with over 300 satisfied customers. The impact of group influence on decision making is described by psychologists as social proof.

Reviews are nudges that leverage the phenomenon of social proof. They change the 'choice architecture' by revealing more information about your options and alleviating some decision stress. It's the reason we scour TripAdvisor reviews before trying out new restaurants. Or skim through product reviews on Amazon before 'adding to cart'. Nearly 55 per cent of consumers read at least four reviews before purchasing a product (Trustpilot, 2020).

By sharing reviews about resources from learners, you can help validate to others that this learning experience is worth the time commitment and is likely to help solve their problem. You can also ask learners to provide their key takeaways from the learning experience, giving others insight into why they engaged in the first place. If most of the feedback highlights a specific takeaway, it's worth including that in your marketing material.

Social proof can also be numerical. A large Twitter follower count, for instance, is an excellent example of it. Showing how many people have viewed, liked or commented on a learning resource can motivate others to engage. You can further nudge by highlighting peers from your tribe who are learning something. Or have a section on your learning platform that highlights the most popular learning resources in their network. A good learning experience platform will have social proof baked in.

Notifications

If you've used any kind of app, you have likely received a notification of some sort. Notifications are a powerful way to deliver intimate, immediate, and contextually relevant information via email, mobile, in-app, and chat tools like Slack and Microsoft Teams.

Here are the types of notifications you can use to engage people throughout the marketing funnel:

- **The ones that send reminders.** These notifications can be effective during the retention and referral stages of the funnel. For example, if someone has booked an online class, you can notify them to join when the start time arrives. Or, if there is an upcoming deadline, send a notification to let the learner know how much time they've got left.

- **The ones that try to get you back.** If you've ever added food to the cart in Uber Eats or Deliveroo but then closed the app, you will have received a notification moments later to check if you wanted to continue to checkout. Similarly, with the help of your learning platform, you can use activity data as notification triggers to nudge people who drop off.

- **The ones that help optimize content.** What if people are dropping off because of the quality of the content? Use notifications to let content creators know. For example, HowNow sends a notification to the course author to let them know if a significant segment of learners drops off at a certain point in the course. This nudges the creator to optimize the content based on quantitative feedback.

- **The ones that provide recommendations.** Send notifications of relevant learning recommendations, rather than a notification every time there is new content. Each notification should serve as an opportunity to inform users and find out what they care about. Based on what you learn, you tailor the notifications further. For example, Netflix uses data to let you know when the new season of a show you have previously watched is out. These notifications can help increase awareness and activation.

- **The ones that help drive referrals.** Once someone has completed a learning experience, follow up with a notification to ask them to share it with their peers or ask them for their feedback and key takeaways. If they forget to do it, remind them the next time they log in to your learning platform or send them a follow-up email with an incentive for giving a review.

Default options

According to Thaler and Sunstein, default options are the most powerful nudge as they do not require any effort by the decision-maker. Defaults can counter inertia and reduce decision fatigue by choosing for the user.

For example, by making your learning platform the default home-page on your browser, you streamline the user journey by removing the employee's decision to go to the learning platform. If you have a learning experience platform that is the front door to your learning ecosystem, you could make its search engine your default internal search, so people never have to think about where they need to go to find learning resources.

Verified content

Enabling internal experts to share their knowledge is fundamental for an organization to learn at speed. However, the risk when people share knowledge is that the content can become outdated and inaccurate. A learning platform with content that is out of date is unreliable and will very quickly lose credibility with your audience.

To combat this, we built a verification engine within HowNow that nudges the content creator to verify that the content they created is valid and accurate. On the flip side, when looking at the content, learners will see a 'verified' symbol. This acts as a nudge for the learner as the symbol enhances the credibility of the content.

Nudging has revolutionized marketing, and it can do the same for how we market learning and development in our organization. It's a tactic that works most effectively when used for good, creating a 'win-win' situation for both companies and individuals. Nudge marketing also requires the support of a modern learning experience platform to automate and scale effortlessly.

You can have the best learning resources in the world. But if you don't couple that with a strategy to spread your story, your learning resources will not go very far. L&D needs to attract employees to learn in the same way marketers grab the attention of busy, distracted consumers. Using marketing, L&D can communicate their value better to individuals and the business and build a culture of continuous learning by creating a consistent demand for it.

What next?

Now we've gone through all the steps in the Lean Learning process, it's time to apply what you've learned. In the final chapter, we'll look at the next steps in your journey to becoming a fast-learning organization.

References

Brit+Co (nd) https://www.brit.co/ (archived at https://perma.cc/6NZH-FDY8)

Chen, J (2021) 36 Essential social media marketing statistics to know for 2021, *SproutSocial*, 3 February, https://sproutsocial.com/insights/social-media-statistics/ (archived at https://perma.cc/BF2E-S5CY)

Dunford, A (2019) *Obviously Awesome: How to nail product positioning so customers get it, buy it, love It*, Ambient Press

Henderson, G (2020) How much time does the average person spend on social media?, *Digital Marketing*, 24 August, https://www.digitalmarketing.org/blog/how-much-time-does-the-average-person-spend-on-social-media (archived at https://perma.cc/4XTC-SAK8)

Herrero, L (2014) Top Influencers 2, Top Leadership 1 (Hierarchical power in the organization is half of the 'peer-to-peer' power), https://leandroherrero.com/top-influencers-2-top-leadership-1-hierarchical-power-in-the-organization-is-half-of-the-peer-to-peer-power/ (archived at https://perma.cc/523L-QWUH)

Hong, J (2021) China's 'Lipstick Brother' Livestreamer sells record $2 billion of goods in one day, *Bloomberg*, 21 October, https://www.bloomberg.com/news/articles/2021-10-21/china-s-lipstick-brother-livestream-has-record-2-billion-day (archived at https://perma.cc/S5VM-WLP6)

Ingraham, C (2017) What's a urinal fly, and what does it have to with winning a Nobel Prize? *Washington Post*, 9 October, https://www.washingtonpost.com/news/wonk/wp/2017/10/09/whats-a-urinal-fly-and-what-does-it-have-to-with-winning-a-nobel-prize/ (archived at https://perma.cc/BQP2-2A7M)

Kolowich Cox, L (2019) The best time to post on Instagram, Facebook, Twitter, LinkedIn, & Pinterest, *HubSpot*, 11 November, https://blog.hubspot.com/marketing/best-times-post-pin-tweet-social-media-infographic (archived at https://perma.cc/Q2GZ-U5WN)

Krans, J (2019) Peek inside Casper's $370 million content marketing universe, *Overthink Group*, 28 March, https://overthinkgroup.com/casper-content-marketing-strategy/ (archived at https://perma.cc/5ZK3-XUKJ)

Marketing Society (nd) Jamal Edwards MBE, https://www.marketingsociety.com/jamal-edwards-mbe (archived at https://perma.cc/Y6FW-7RZV)

Protocol 80 (2020) 2021 Inbound Marketing Stats on the Power of Call-to-Action Buttons, 10 November, https://www.protocol80.com/blog/2019-cta-statistics (archived at https://perma.cc/5V87-E7WV)

Shah et al (2019) Nudging for good: Using behavioral science to improve government outcomes, *Deloitte Insights*, https://www2.deloitte.com/us/en/insights/industry/public-sector/government-trends/2020/government-nudge-thinking.html (archived at https://perma.cc/XXW3-XPM3)

Sinek, S (2009) How great leaders inspire action, *TED*, https://www.ted.com/talks/simon_sinek_how_great_leaders_inspire_action?language=en (archived at https://perma.cc/N7V7-26YN)

Statista (2021) Most valuable brands worldwide in 2021, 12 October, https://www.statista.com/statistics/264875/brand-value-of-the-25-most-valuable-brands (archived at https://perma.cc/L3NS-VEYL)

Thaler, R and Sunstein, C (2009) *Nudge: Improving decisions about health, wealth and happiness*, Penguin

Toms (nd) Our Story, https://www.toms.com/uk/about-toms.html (archived at https://perma.cc/4U53-TH3G)

Trustpilot (2020) 4 Things every business owner should know about the state of reviews, https://uk.business.trustpilot.com/reviews/build-trusted-brand/4-things-every-business-owner-should-know-about-the-state-of-reviews (archived at https://perma.cc/9SKZ-FWXZ)

Conclusion: Always winning

The value of an idea lies in the using of it.

THOMAS EDISON

As I write this, the metaverse is having a moment. Originally coined by author Neal Stephenson in his 1992 science fiction novel *Snow Crash* and now anticipated to be the next internet, the metaverse is a shared, immersive world made of augmented, virtual and mixed reality.

We don't yet know what the metaverse will look like or when it will eventually fully arrive. The expectation is you will be able to do everything on the metaverse – connect, shop, create, learn, work and do new types of things that we can't yet do with our computers or phones.

The metaverse is yet another manifestation of exponential change. The fastest learners are already seizing the opportunities and winning. Even the home of Mickey Mouse and Princess Elsa, Disney, has revealed it is planning to join the likes of Meta (formerly Facebook) and Microsoft in the metaverse (Wright, 2022).

Other companies are still trying to grasp the concept or, even worse, being dismissive like the early naysayers of the internet. Speed of learning will again determine the new winners and losers. The purpose of this book is to help you help your organization win in this fast-changing and uncertain world.

You may have heard of the noble families fighting over who rules the seven kingdoms of Westeros? If not, spoilers ahead. In *Game of Thrones*, the different leaders battle to sit on the 'Iron Throne', whilst none of them realize that there is a greater threat to their existence coming from the Army of the Dead from the North – and their tried and tested methods will not work against this common enemy.

However, our protagonist, Jon Snow, is aware of the greater threat and realizes that they will need to realign their mission, shift their mindset and implement new methods to win. Snow then attempts to get the warring families to prepare for the real change that is about to descend on them. You're Jon Snow, and that's why you've read this book. One step in the right direction is all it takes to change your destination. This is your first step.

Like Jon Snow, we must first realign our mission. Our mission is to enable our teams to learn as fast as the world is changing, maybe even faster. Then we need to shift our mindset to love the problem and have a bias towards action. We must be open to failing fast and continuously improve and tackle the riskiest assumption first. We must measure what we want to achieve, prioritize outcome over output, empower the team, and eliminate waste.

Now we change our methods. Using Lean Learning, we can connect the right learning resource with the right person at the right time to drive the right impact. The process starts with identifying, understanding and clearly defining the right problem using the Customer Discovery approach. Then, like sketching a business plan on a napkin, we collaboratively create an L&D strategy using the Learning Canvas.

Once you have a plan, it's time to turn your L&D strategy into a learning experience you can start to test. Begin with building a dynamic learning ecosystem that brings together open resources, collaborative learning, knowledge sharing, job aids, coaching, mentoring, online courses and radically flipped classrooms.

Using data-driven push learning and curation-powered pull learning, personalize learning at scale. Define the influencers of the moments that matter so you can connect learning in the real-world context. Embed measurement into learning experiences to generate proof of knowledge, skill and performance.

Map the ideas for learning experiences using the Learning Experience Bullseye framework. Using the ICE approach, we prioritize the ideas and define the Minimum Valuable Learning. By running Lean Learning sprints, we go through the steps of the Learning Flywheel to test and iterate the MVL until we achieve learning-challenge fit.

Once you've achieved learning-challenge fit, you use the L&D marketing funnel to scale the learning experience to everyone who needs it and retain them until you drive measurable performance improvement.

Lean Learning is an alchemy of mental models, frameworks and tactics used by the most disruptive companies in the world to enable learning at speed. I hope this playbook has shown that you too can apply similar ideas to build a fast-learning organization.

In Lean Learning, the finish line is performance, not learning. So this book is just the beginning of your learning experience loop. The next step is to practise what you've learned. You can find all of the templates discussed in the book at gethownow.com.

Don't overthink it. Just start with a small experiment. Gather feedback to find out what worked and what didn't. Share what you learn with peers inside and outside of your company, and then go again.

Ten best practices

Having tried and tested the frameworks in this book with organizations big and small, here are ten best practices that might be helpful to guide you along the way:

1 **Use proof to get buy-in.** Lean Learning can be a significant change to how you currently work. If your teammates don't buy in, then test fast and let reality convince them. You're not going to win by arguing; you'll just wind up working alone.

2 **Foster strong team relationships.** Stay consistent by reinforcing team spirit, collaboration and communication throughout the project from ideation to completion. Have a social after every Lean Learning sprint.

3 **Defer critical decisions.** Wait until the last responsible moment to make a decision. The last responsible moment is defined as the moment you've learned enough about a decision to act on it.

4 **Sticky notes are your friend.** One idea per sticky note. Use thick pens to constrain the amount you can write, or big font if you're doing it virtually. Write so that your teammates can understand it.

5 **Celebrate failure.** Appreciate colleagues who try new things and fail. Invalidated an assumption? Group cheer. Killed the whole learning strategy? Put it in the project graveyard and pop the champagne. Failure moves you closer to your desired outcome.

6 **Work with your customer.** Listen actively to the customer. Listen to their gasps and sighs. Listen to their emotions. If you can watch them try to solve their problem for themselves, even better.

7 **Beware of the vanity metric.** Change what you're measuring if it doesn't tell you how it improved someone's knowledge, skills proficiency or performance. Prioritize the metric that signals your outcome rather than one that shows the output.

8 **Lead by example.** Internalize and model the behaviours and mindsets of Lean Learning so that others can learn and grow by your example.

9 **Don't waste time in meetings.** Meetings should be focused and concise, with a timekeeper to keep you on track. If the meeting is not adding value, it's a waste and should be removed.

10 **Tear down silos.** Learning is not one department's job. Everyone must take responsibility for it. It takes collective, interdisciplinary effort to create the best conditions for continuous, performance-driven learning.

Learning at speed doesn't just win the race; it gains a head start for the next one. But it's important to point out that learning at speed is not a zero-sum game. There don't need to be losers for the fastest learners to win. It's not about beating others. Winners focus on winning, losers focus on winners.

Winners strive to grow, innovate and add value to the world around them, but not at a cost to anyone else. When more organizations learn to learn at speed, the better it will be for all of us because the sooner people get the right skills, knowledge and mindset, the faster we can solve the biggest problems in the world.

And everybody wins.

References

Stephenson, N (1992) *Snow Crash*, Penguin

Wright, K. (2022) Disney patents technology for a theme park metaverse, *Coin Telegraph*, 10 January, https://cointelegraph.com/news/disney-patents-technology-for-a-theme-park-metaverse (archived at https://perma.cc/X858-V9SP)

INDEX

3M 113

action, bias towards 24–26
active learning 87–88
ADDIE (Assess, Design, Develop, Implement, Evaluate) approach by L&D teams 18
agile approach 3, 4, 28, 34, 62, 155–56 *see also* minimum valuable learning (MVL)
Airbnb 123
Alibaba 189
Allen & Overy 84–85
Amazon 26
Andreessen, Marc 137, 138
Apple 179
Arcadia Group 1
ASOS 1
assumptions, tackle the riskiest assumptions first 30–31
audio courses 86

Bezos, Jeff 26
Bitcoin 2
Blank, Steve 46
Blockbuster 23–24
Bloom's Taxonomy 88
Bloomberg 78
Boeing 85
brand identity 183–84
brand mission 181
brand name 182–83
brand personality 184–85
brand story 182
brand tone of voice 184–85
brand values 181–82
BrewDog 3
Brit + Co 181
Buffer 25, 189
Business Model Canvas 60
business strategy, alignment of learning strategy 147–48
Butterfield, Stewart 137–38

calls to action (CTAs) 197–98
Canva 86, 188
Carnegie, Dale 67–68
Casper 175–76
Caterpillar 85
change
    accelerating pace of 1, 2
    exponential growth bias 6
    learning fast and realigning our mission 205–07
    underestimation of the rate of 6
checklists 82
Chesky, Brian 123
Christensen, Clayton M 43
CIPD 78
ClickUp 167
Clubhouse 86
coaching 83–85
cohort-based courses (CBCs) 80–81
collaborative learning 78–81
community platforms 147
company announcements 152
compliance-driven learning culture 14
content authoring platforms 146
content creation 95
content libraries 147
content marketing 175–76
context of training and learning 13
continuous improvement mindset 28–30
continuous learning
    continuous measurement required 119
    Lean Learning sprints 155–73
Covid-19 pandemic 1, 2
    impact on viewing habits 12
    impact on Zoom 43–44
    influence on learning needs 109
    loss of knowledge transfer among employees 79
    surge in startups 3
    usage of communication tools 105
Credit Karma 3

crises, incubators for startups 3
Croll, Alistair 111
curation of learning content 95–97
Customer Development 4
customer discovery interviews 46–56
    after the interview 55
    before the interview 53
    how to find people to interview 47–49
    how to start the interview 53
    interview process 52–55
    prepare your questions beforehand 53
    problem discovery 54
    set the scene 53
    warm up 54
    what questions to ask 49–52
    who to talk to 47
    wrap up 55
customer discovery process 46–56
customer segments 64, 66

decision fatigue 95
decision-making process, mindset change 26
default options, nudge marketing 201
Depop 79–80
design thinking 4
digital adoption platforms (DAPs) 83, 105
digital credentials 147
digital performance support 82–83
Disney 205
disruptive innovation 43
diversity 85–86
Dollar Shave Club (DSC) 41
DreamWorks 11
Dubin, Michael 41
Dunford, April 195
Dweck, Carol 22

Edison, Thomas 205
Edmonson, Amy 148–49
Edwards, Jamal 192
Einstein, Albert 23
electronic performance support systems 105
Ellis, Sean 133
employee-driven 'pull' learning 94–97
employee empowerment 35–36
employee performance, impact of
    training 16–17
evaluation of learning impact, traditional
    methods used by L&D 112
exponential growth bias 6

Facebook 189
fail fast approach 3, 26–28
failure, role in continuous improvement 29

Fake, Caterina 11
FAQs (frequently asked questions), use of
    templates 82
fastest learners, advantages for 1, 2
feedback
    on the learner 142–43
    on the learning experience 143
    role in continuous improvement 29
    tools 147
first principles thinking
    definition 58–59
    how to apply it to workplace
        learning 59–60
fixed mindset 22
Flickr 11
flowcharts 83
FOMO (Fear of Missing Out) 198
forcing functions 151–53
Ford, Henry 58
FT 78

Game of Thrones 206
Gates, Bill 22, 95
Gawande, Atul 84
Gebbia, Joe 123
General Electric 85
Gillette 41
global financial crisis (2008) 3
Gmail 29
Godin, Seth 75, 80–81
Google 30, 113, 192
    g2g employee-to-employee network 79
Google Explore 105
Google Keyword Planner tool 193–94
Groupon 3
Grove, Andy 5
growth mindset 22
Gutenberg, Johannes 58
GymShark 79–80

hackathons 80
Halligan, Brian 91–92
heuristics 198
high-leverage activity 5
Hootsuite 189
how-to resources 78
HowNow 4, 77, 79–80, 87, 96, 105, 118,
    147, 192, 193, 194, 200, 201, 207
HubSpot 91–92

IDEO 78
inbound marketing 92
inclusion 85–86
industry-specific learning resources 77

influencer marketing 189–92
Instagram 12, 86, 186, 187, 189
Intercom 62

job aids 81–83
job stories 62–63
job to be done, mapping the learning
    strategy to 44
Jobs-To-Be-Done (JTBD) framework 43–46
    focus on the job to be done, not the
        learner 44
    how to find the jobs to be done 45–46
    learning experiences are not the job,
        they're the product 44–45
    there are many ways to get the job
        done 45

Kaizen (continuous improvement) 28
kanban board 167, 168
Kao, Wes 81
Katzenberg, Jeffrey 11
keyword research 193–94
Klement, Alan 62
Kniberg, Henrik 155
knowledge bases 79–80, 146
knowledge sharing, within and across
    organizations 78–81

L&D see Learning and Development
Lean Canvas 60–61
Lean Learning
    adapting successful startup strategies 4
    definition of 17–18
    development of the approach 4
    features of 75–76
    mindset 22–37
    practise what you have learned 207–09
    process leading to improved
        performance 206–07
    ten best practices 207–09
    why it matters 16–18
Lean Learning sprints
    assembling the right team for the
        sprint 158–60
    avoid going over time 165
    avoid idea attachment 165
    benefits of 157
    benefits of an agile approach 155–56
    concept of sprint cycles 155–56
    daily standups 169–70
    definition of 156–57
    how to run 160–73
    idea mapping 164–66
    just enough research 166

prepare for testing 170
roles in the sprint team 158–60
setup for success 163
sprint backlog 167
sprint planning 166–68
sprint retrospective 172–73
sprint review 171–72
Sprint Zero 162–63
Stage 1 (choose your strategy) 160–63
Stage 2 (map your learning
    experience) 164–68
Stage 3 (testing your MVL) 169–70
Stage 4 (evaluate your strategy) 171–73
value vs effort matrix 162–63
Lean manufacturing, Toyota 34
Lean methodology 28
The Lean Startup (Ries) 1, 30, 125, 144
Lean Startup model 4, 139
learner engagement, radically flipped
    classrooms 87–88
Learning and Development (L&D)
    adapting successful startup strategies 4
    managers' dissatisfaction with 12–13
    marketing funnel 176–79
    reasons why it fails 4
    similarity to a failing startup 12–13
    solving the right problem 42–43
    traditional ADDIE approach 18
    what went wrong at Quibi 11–12
    where it is going wrong 13
learning at speed
    necessity of 1, 2
    underestimation of the rate of change 6
learning brand building 179–86
    using social media 186–89
learning by doing 24–26
Learning Canvas 60–73, 117, 139, 144, 162,
    196–97
    actions you need to take 65, 66–70
    costs 71, 72
    customer segments 64, 66
    development of the concept 60–61
    how to create your Learning
        Canvas 61–73
    job stories 62–63
    key metrics 70–71, 72
    key resources 68–70
    knowledge 67
    mindset 67
    outcome 70, 72
    partners and stakeholders to collaborate
        with 68, 69
    problem hypothesis 62–63
    skills 67–68

Learning Canvas (*Continued*)
  solution 67–68, 69
  the HOW 65, 66–70
  the WHAT 70–73
  the WHY 62–65
  value proposition 64–65, 66
Learning-Challenge Fit
  definition of 138–39
  how to achieve it 139–53
  iterative process 139
  Learning Flywheel 139–53
learning content, optimizing for
  searching 192–95
learning culture in organizations 13
  impact of training on employee
    performance 16–17
  new approach of Lean Learning 17–18
  types of 14–16
learning ecosystem 75–88
  changes in workplace learning 76–77
  coaching and mentoring 83–86
  collaborative learning 78–81
  features of a dynamic learning
    ecosystem 77–88
  how-to resources 78
  industry insights 77
  job aids 81–83
  knowledge sharing within and across
    organizations 78–81
  learner engagement in virtual
    classrooms 87–88
  learning media/providers 78
  online courses 86–87
  open learning resources 77–78
  performance support 81–83
  personal learning budgets 86–87
  radically flipped classrooms 87–88
  right resources 75–76
  thought leadership 78
  wider role for L&D professionals
    76–77, 88
Learning Experience (LX) loop 139, 140
Learning Experience Bullseye (LXB)
  Framework 128–35, 144, 164
Learning Experience Design (LXD)
  loop 139, 140
learning experience platforms
  (LXP) 105, 146
learning experiences, positioning of 195–97
Learning Flywheel 139–53, 157, 159
  how to turn the flywheel faster 145–53
  iterative process 139–45
  overcoming inertia 145–53

  tackling unwanted friction 145–53
learning from failure 26–28
learning management systems (LMS) 59, 146
learning media/providers 78
learning out loud 152
learning pacts 153
learning resources *see* learning ecosystem
learning strategy 139
learning strategy development 57–73
  alignment with business strategy 147–48
  using the Learning Canvas 60–73
learning tech stack 146–47
Leboeuf, Michael 57
Levitt, Theodore 43
Li Jiaqi 189
LinkedIn 189, 191
Linklaters 86
Loom 86
Lorentzon, Martin 41

manager check-in 152–53
managers, lack of meaningful involvement in
  training 15
marketing 175–202
  building a learning brand 179–86
  calls to action (CTAs) 197–98
  content marketing 175–76
  inbound marketing 92
  influencer marketing 189–92
  L&D marketing funnel 176–79
  nudge marketing 198–202
  outbound marketing 92
  product positioning 195–97
  search engine optimization
    (SEO) 192–95
  using social media 186–89
Maurya, Ash 60
measurement
  driver of change 31–32
  impact of learning 111–19
MEDDPICC methodology 118
mentoring 83–84, 85–86
Meta (formerly Facebook) 205
metaverse concept 205
microlearning 86
Microsoft 2, 205
  hackathons 80
  turnaround of 21–22
Microsoft Teams 105, 200
mindset
  fixed mindset 22
  growth mindset 22
mindset shift

bias towards action 24–26
continuous improvement 28–30
eliminate wasteful practices 34–35
empower the team 35–36
fail fast, fail often approach 26–28
Lean Learning mindset 22–37
love the problem 23–24
Microsoft turnaround 21–22
outcome over outputs 32–34
perception of risk 25–26
tackle the riskiest assumptions
    first 30–31
understand the problem 23–24
you get what you measure 31–32
Minerva Project 88
minimum valuable learning (MVL)
avoid over-building 127
avoid over-minimizing 128
benefits of starting with an MVL 125–27
definition of 124–25
focus on what matters 126
go slow to go fast 127
how to design an MVL 128–35
increase speed of learning 125–26
Learning Experience Bullseye (LXB)
    Framework 128–35
minimize uncertainties and risk 125
pay attention to feedback 128
pitfalls to avoid when building an
    MVL 127–28
win stakeholder buy-in 126
see also Learning-Challenge Fit
minimum viable product (MVP) 123
mobile learning 146
moments that matter (MTM)
activity context of learning 107
'aha' moment 102–03
definition of 102
external factors/context 108–09
influence of technology 105–06
influence of the physical
    environment 104
macro-moment that matters 103
micro-moment that matters 103
organizational culture/context 108
relevance of learning and 102–03
shaping performance in 101–09
six influencers of MTM 103–09
time context for learning 106
types of 103
MOOCs (Massive Open Online
    Courses) 80, 86
Mowen, Stella 101
Mui, Chunka 123

Musk, Elon 57–58, 59
Mycoskie, Blake 182

Nadella, Satya 21–22
nano-courses 86
Netflix 12, 23–24, 95
notifications, nudge marketing 200–01
NPR 155
nudge marketing
default options 201
features of 198–202
notifications 200–01
social proofs 199–200
verified content 201
Nuzum, Eric 155

Ogilvy, David 175
on-demand economy 101
online courses 86–87
on-screen support and guidance 82–83
open learning resources 77–78
organization-driven 'push' learning 92–94
organizations, need to learn fast for
    survival 2
Osterwalder, Alex 60
outbound marketing 92
outcome-first mindset 32–34

peer-to-peer learning 79
performance, shaping in the moments that
    matter 101–09
performance improvement
measuring the impact of learning 111–19
proof of performance 115–119, 142, 143
performance review 84–85
performance support systems 105, 146
job aids 81–83
persevering 144
Pershing 85
personal learning budgets 86–87
personalized learning 91–98
curation of learning content 94–97
employee-driven 'pull' learning 94–98
organization-driven 'push'
    learning 92–94, 97–98
pivoting 144
Pixar studios 165
podcasts 86
presentations 152
problem-first approach, driver of continuous
    improvement 29
problem solving 41–56
bias towards action 24–26
finding the right problem to solve 41–42

problem solving (*Continued*)
  global maximum solution 23–23
  Jobs-To-Be-Done (JTBD)
    framework 43–46
  Lean Learning sprints 155–73
  local maximum solution 23–24
  love the problem 23–24
  mindset shift 22–37
  solving the right problem 42–43
  understand the problem 23–24
process-driven learning culture 14
product-market fit 137, 138
product positioning 195–97
Project Management Institute 78
projects 152
proof of impact, measuring performance
    improvement 111–19
proof of knowledge 112, 141
proof of performance 115–119, 142, 143
  continuous measurement 119
  qualitative measurement 117–19
  quantitative measurement 115–17, 118–19
  triangulation of qualitative and
    quantitative methods 118–19
proof of skill 113–15, 142, 143
psychological safety
  impact on team performance 148–50
  ways to build it in a team 149–50
pull learning 94–98
push learning 92–94, 97–98

QR codes 83
Quibi, what went wrong 11–12
quiz builders 147

Rampton, John 91
reasoning by analogy 59
recognition and rewards 150–51
relevance of learning *see* moments that
    matter
reporting 153
request for proposal (RFP) 59
reskilling of employees, need for 2
resources, website for templates 207
Resy 3
reverse mentoring 85–86
reviews, nudge marketing 199
rewards and recognition 150–51
Ries, Eric 1, 30, 125, 144
risk
  perceptions of 25–26
  related to inaction 25–26
  tackle the riskiest assumptions first 30–31

SBTV 192
Scrum framework 155
search engine optimization (SEO) 192–95
self-paced learning 86–87
Shah, Dharmesh 91–92
Sinek, Simon 180–81
skills assessment tools 146
skills-driven learning culture 15–16
Slack 3, 80, 105, 137–38, 200
social media
  management tools 189
  putting it to work 186–89
social proofs, nudge marketing 199–200
software development, approaches to 34
SpaceX 57–58
Sprout Social 189
startups
  emerging from crises 3
  learning to learn fast from 3
  reasons why they fail 4
  surge related to the Covid-19
    pandemic 3
Stephenson, Neal 205
Sunstein, Cass 198, 201
survey tools 147

tacit knowledge 79–80
team performance, psychological safety
    and 148–50
teams, empowerment of 35–36
technology, learning tech stack 146–47
TED talks 78, 84, 180–81
Teller, Astro 30
templates 82
Tesla 179
testing assumptions, minimum valuable
    learning (MVL) 123–35
Thaler, Richard 198, 201
thought leadership 78
TikTok 12, 187, 188
timing of learning *see* moments that matter
Toms Shoes 182
Toyota, Lean manufacturing 34
training programmes
  contribution to workplace learning 76
  see also Learning and Development
    (L&D)
Trello 167
Twitter 187, 188, 189, 199
Twitter Spaces 86

Uber 3
Unilever 41

upskilling of employees, need for 2
user stories 62

value proposition 64–65, 66
value vs effort matrix 162–63
Venmo 3
verified content, nudge marketing 201
virtual classrooms 146
    learner engagement 87–88
voice notes 86

Walsh, Bill 21
wasteful practices, elimination of 34–35

Waterfall project management approach 34
WhatsApp 3
Whitman, Meg 11
Whittinghill, Joe 22
wikis 79–80, 146
workplace learning *see* learning ecosystem

YouTube 192

Zoom 105
    impact of the Covid-19 pandemic
        43–44
Zoom fatigue 87

CPSIA information can be obtained
at www.ICGtesting.com
Printed in the USA
JSHW060945240622
27371JS00014B/537